GARDENS
of the
LAKE DISTRICT

TIM LONGVILLE

GARDENS
of the
LAKE DISTRICT

TIM LONGVILLE

Photography by Val Corbett

Frances Lincoln Ltd
4 Torriano Mews
Torriano Avenue
London NW5 2RZ
www.franceslincoln.com

A catalogue record for this book is available from the
British Library.
ISBN 13: 978-0-7112-2713-2
Printed and bound in China

1 2 3 4 5 6 7 8 9

Garden openings under the National Gardens Scheme are
listed in *The Yellow Book: NGS Gardens Open for Charity*,
published annually by the National Gardens Scheme.

We are grateful to all the owners, creators, custodians and
gardeners without whose generous help and hospitality
creating this book would have been impossible. Over the
years many magazine editors have given us space in their
pages for our words about and photographs of Cumbrian
gardens. We are grateful to them all – particularly Keith
Richardson, former editor of *Cumbria Life*, who provided a
regular home in its pages for our articles for almost a decade.

PREVIOUS PAGES Rydal Hall, the newly restored garden
by Thomas Mawson.

RIGHT Holehird in winter.

CONTENTS

6 INTRODUCTION

10 HOLKER HALL, CARK IN CARTMEL

16 YEWBARROW HOUSE, GRANGE-OVER-SANDS

24 PEAR TREE COTTAGE, BURTON-IN-KENDAL

32 HOLME CRAG, WITHERSLACK

36 HALECAT, WITHERSLACK

42 LEVENS HALL

52 SIZERGH CASTLE

56 MUNCASTER CASTLE, RAVENGLASS

64 BRANTWOOD, CONISTON

72 HIGH CLEABARROW, WINDERMERE

80 WINDY HALL, WINDERMERE

86 HIGH CROSS LODGE, TROUTBECK

94 HOLEHIRD, WINDERMERE

100 BROCKHOLE, WINDERMERE

106 STAGSHAW, AMBLESIDE

110 MATTHEW HOW, TROUTBECK

118 COPT HOWE, GREAT LANGDALE

126 RYDAL HALL AND RYDAL MOUNT

134 PARCEY HOUSE, HARTSOP

140 GRANGE FARM, NORTH CUMBRIA

146 SCARTHWAITE, GRANGE-IN-BORROWDALE

152 BRACKENBURN, MANESTY, BORROWDALE

158 GREENCROFT HOUSE, GREAT STRICKLAND

164 DALEMAIN, PENRITH

172 THE OLD RECTORY, DEAN

176 FELLSIDE, MILLBECK

180 MIREHOUSE, KESWICK

188 WINDERWATH, TEMPLE SOWERBY

194 ACORN BANK, TEMPLE SOWERBY

200 CHAPELSIDE, MUNGRISDALE

206 BEAUHILL, PENRITH

212 HUTTON-IN-THE-FOREST, SKELTON, NEAR PENRITH

218 NUNWICK HALL, GREAT SALKELD

224 THE MILL HOUSE, SEBERGHAM

230 CORBY CASTLE, GREAT CORBY

236 GARTH HOUSE, BRAMPTON

242 CAIRNBECK, NEAR IRTHINGTON

248 OTHER GARDENS
Buckbarrow House, Gosforth; Cardew Lodge, Dalston;
Gatesgarth, Watermillock; Glen Artney, Armathwaite;
Graythwaite Hall, near Ulverston; Lake House, Capernwray;
Morland House, Morland; Quarry Hill House, Mealsgate;
Rose Castle, Dalston; Roundhill, Easedale;
Wood Ghyll, Crosthwaite; Wood Hall, Cockermouth

253 MAP

254 INDEX

INTRODUCTION

Visitors from other parts of Britain or other parts of the world often seem to have preconceptions about the Lake District. Doesn't it have lots and lots of rain, they ask? The winters are endless and bone-chillingly cold, aren't they? Wouldn't only a committed masochist try to make a garden there?

The Lake District certainly doesn't suffer much from drought, but how much rain you get depends on where you are. If you are in the rain shadow of a mountain, you can often get surprisingly little rain. And in gardening terms the Lake District's combination of (let us be tactful) reliable moisture with a generally peaty soil provides ideal conditions for growing an enormous range of acid-loving plants, from tree-sized rhododendrons and eucryphias down to miniature trilliums, erythroniums and primulas. And one group of plants above all thrives in the Lake District: ferns. Indeed, the British specialist society devoted to ferns – the British Pteridological Society – began here, when Victorian enthusiasts discovered and delighted in the many forms growing wild in Borrowdale. Unsurprisingly, ferns feature extensively in many Lake District gardens, such as Nan Hicks' sophisticated cottage garden at Grange-in-Borrowdale.

Given the last decade's run of mild winters, it isn't even true – at least for the time being – that winters here are particularly long or cold. Indeed, there are parts of Cumbria, beyond the central 'spine' of mountains and lakes of the Lake District proper, which hardly ever have cold winters. (Here I should say that although the title of this book is *Gardens of the Lake District*, I have in fact selected gardens not just from within the Lake District but from throughout the county of Cumbria.) To the south of Cumbria, among the lower fells and the farmland leading down to the northern shores of Morecambe Bay, the climate is drier and warmer, with a much wider range of soil conditions, and as a result it is possible for gardeners there to grow a surprisingly wide and rewarding palette of plants. The same is true to the north, in the rolling countryside between Penrith and Carlisle or in the lovely Eden Valley, where traditional English country gardens flourish, overflowing with lush herbaceous planting. And it is often forgotten that Cumbria has a coastline – a western coastline at that. All of it, from the far south around Grange-over-Sands to the

The pool in the lower garden at Holehird in winter.

far north around Bowness-on-Solway, has conditions closer to those of north Devon or north Cornwall than to those of central Cumbria. Winter temperatures rarely fall below −3°C, and from Victorian times onwards, keen gardeners have taken advantage of this to create gardens in an improbably Mediterranean or even subtropical style.

And of course the Lake District has another advantage for gardeners: the lakes and mountains are not only beautiful in themselves but make unbeatable bits of 'borrowed landscape'. As such they act as dramatic backdrops to many of Cumbria's best gardens.

Once you have realized all that, it becomes less surprising to discover that Cumbria has a long history of distinguished gardens in many different styles. There is the famous and rare survivor at Levens Hall of the formal gardens of the seventeenth century. There are some of the earliest and most remarkable examples of Picturesque gardens from the later seventeenth and early eighteenth centuries, such as those at Rydal Hall near Ambleside and Corby Castle near Carlisle. Rydal Hall is also a good example of the way the county's older gardens have often developed over the centuries, layer after layer being added in fascinatingly different styles.

The nineteenth century, here as elsewhere in Britain, saw more gardens than ever before being created, in a profusion of different styles. Woodland and parkland gardens, for example, such as those at Hutton-in-the-Forest, Dalemain and Holker Hall, were given elaborate shrub and herbaceous 'extensions'. Several of Cumbria's most delightful gardens from that period were made by writers who at the same time were making the county's wild natural landscape famous all over the world. Fortunately, Wordsworth's garden at Rydal Mount and Ruskin's at Brantwood still retain much of their original appearance and atmosphere.

There were two forms of nineteenth- and early twentieth-century garden which were particularly characteristic of Cumbria. The first was the grand rhododendron garden: the county's outstanding example of that – indeed, one of the most outstanding examples in Britain – is the more than 70 acres of the Muncaster Castle garden. The second and even more peculiarly Cumbrian form was the garden of a super-cottage-cum-mini-country-house. Such houses were often commissioned by a Lancashire business-man, designed either by Dan Gibson or C.A. Voysey and surrounded by extensive gardens by (or in the style of) the Windermere-based designer Thomas Mawson. Sometimes

The tiny formal front garden of Matthew How. Its undulating boundary hedge tries to imitate the tops of the High Street fells on the skyline.

Mawson produced sophisticated oversized cottage gardens, sometimes (as at Brockhole and Rydal Hall) grandly ostentatious formal ones, but always he demonstrated a real appreciation of how best to fit a garden into Cumbria's dramatic landscape.

A few inspired enthusiasts have continued to create gardens on that sort of large and elaborate scale. Jonathan Denby at Yewbarrow House in Grange-over-Sands and David Tate at Garth House in Brampton have both done so within the past decade. However, the twentieth century was – and the twenty-first shows every sign of continuing to be – above all the century of the smaller 'plantsman's garden'. Cumbria has a rich array of such gardens, varying from Hugh Barr's precipitous hillside haven above Penrith, in which rare New Zealand alpines flourish, to Kay Jefferson's spectacular country garden at Sebergham with its borders full of carefully planned colour combinations.

Those several centuries of changing styles mean that this book includes three dozen very different gardens. For each I have provided an account of both its history and the 'philosophy' behind its creation. Realizing that what readers who are keen gardeners want more than anything else is detailed information on plants, I have also wherever possible included the owner's or head gardener's selection of personal favourites, often with their explanation of the plants' virtues and the specific purposes and situations for which they are suited. Inevitably, there are some repetitions in these selections, but these repetitions are useful, since they indicate plants admired by very different gardeners dealing with very different situations and working in very different styles.

Finally, the simultaneously happy-but-sad fact is that Cumbria has such a rich garden heritage that it is impossible to cover all of it in a single book. The gardens included here are a purely personal selection and I apologize to the curators and creators of the county's many other fine examples, which have been excluded only by limitations of space. Brief descriptions of some of these are given on pages 248–52.

TIM LONGVILLE

HOLKER HALL, CARK IN CARTMEL

The garden at Holker Hall, close to the coast in the far south of Cumbria, is fortunate in being run by two passionate and knowledgeable owners and managed by a young, energetic and committed head gardener. In addition, because of the garden's scale (it covers 55 acres), its long history and gradual development, and because the owners, Lord and Lady Cavendish, have separate if overlapping areas of interest and responsibility in the garden, Holker is really several gardens in one. What visitors tend to see first – and the part of the garden which is most immediately eye-catching – are the several stylistically distinct areas of the grand formal gardens around the house. Beyond that, though, lie the more subtle charms of Holker's even more extensive and extremely distinguished Woodland Garden.

The two major 'house' gardens, the Elliptical Garden and the Summer Garden, were redesigned some years ago by Lady Cavendish because she felt that, as the areas which visitors tended to encounter first, they needed to provide the greatest possible impact over the longest possible season. The Elliptical Garden (the name comes from the visual sleight-of-hand involved in the creation of its centrepiece, which seems to be circular but in fact is not) contains four main borders. These are colour-themed, at the moment in yellow, mauve, pink and purple, and are backed up by a series of enormous and impressive planters, constructed from slate from the estate's own quarries. To ensure that the beds and planters provide interest for as long as possible the plants in both have to be changed several times during the course of a season. This involves a huge number of plants and many hours' work for all the gardeners, and the 'change overs' have to be effected with as little disturbance as possible to the visiting public.

Another challenge in these areas for head gardener Paul Wilson and his team is the fact that the garden, especially around the house, keeps changing and expanding in design as well as in content. That is partly because it has to if the garden is continually to provide the visiting public with something new, and partly because Lord and Lady Cavendish are so in love with their garden that they just can't resist playing with it. This involves the

The cascade and the fountain, flanked by *Rhododendron arboreum*.

Cavendishes and their head gardener in many three-way discussions – at any given moment the subject might be this season's colours in the Summer Garden's beds, where to put a new plant in the woodland or how to redesign a whole area. The Cavendishes' urge to try something new – and better – means that for a long-established garden this is a remarkably 'mobile' one.

Lord and Lady Cavendish are sometimes happy to return an area to what was there before. For example, after a period of experimenting there with other styles, the area known as the Sunken Garden has been returned to a more traditional arrangement, in which roses are supported by herbaceous underplanting. At other times, though, change involves a completely new design.

For example, down in the Wildflower Meadow beyond the Summer Garden, a relatively new addition is a striking labyrinth designed by Jim Buchanan and Lady Cavendish, containing twelve pillars of slate, again from the estate's own quarries. It was sited here because, Lady Cavendish explains, they felt that as a new form of an ancient tradition the labyrinth made a fitting link between the formality of the house gardens and the informality of the parkland and natural landscape beyond.

The formal gardens aim at – and, in the most stylish way, achieve – instant pizzazz, the gardening equivalent of 'shock and awe'. They are examples of grand gardening on a grand scale. The scale of the Woodland Garden is even larger, consisting of dozens

of grassy acres criss-crossed by innumerable walks which wind among informal plantings of hundreds if not thousands of trees and shrubs. Yet its effect is very different: gentle, relaxing, laid-back, contemplative. The result of two hundred years of discriminating planting, it is particularly rewarding for gardening connoisseurs. It is possible – and intensely pleasurable – to spend hours finding and studying its innumerable distinguished plants. These include the National Collection of the whole family of the *Styracaceae*, which embraces as well as the *Styrax* the *Halesia*, the *Pterostyrax* and rarities such as two recent additions to the collection, *Huodendron tibeticum* and *Melliodendron xylocarpum*. Like the latter, many of the rarities grown here are on the edges of

OPPOSITE The entrance to the formal gardens.

ABOVE The house seen from the formal gardens. The plants include silver weeping pears (*Pyrus salicifolia* 'Pendula'), underplanted with tulips and forget-me-nots.

hardiness in most British gardens but Holker's west-coast climate allows success with trees and shrubs which are seldom seen in the north of England.

Though both Cavendishes are deeply involved in the continuing planting here, this area is Lord Cavendish's own particular private passion. 'In the height of the season I really like to come

The Wildflower Meadow, now also home to Jim Buchanan's new labyrinth of slate pillars.

round twice a day, just to keep track of what's going on,' he says. Not that it would be easy to say when the height of the season is here, since the Woodland Garden is full of spectacular flowers, from the early-spring-flowering magnolias, camellias and rhododendrons through to early-autumn-flowering eucryphias. Even after that it still offers extensive and dramatic late autumn colour.

I would suggest, though, that the end of May or beginning of June would be a particularly good time to visit. That is when Holker's weekend-long Garden Festival takes place and the Woodland Garden's vast range of spring-flowering trees and shrubs is likely to be at its very best. The Garden Festival began about ten years ago. 'We used to do lots of events here but many of them weren't things we had our hearts in,' Lady Cavendish explains. 'So we decided to try to create a sort of flagship event, something which would be connected to what Holker has to offer and to our passion for plants and gardens.' Her husband explains

its aims – and indeed their aims in the whole garden. 'I'm not an elitist. Well, no, that's not true. I am. But I'm an inclusive elitist, not an exclusive one. I don't want to keep people out; I want to get more and more people in. I want them to make more interesting gardens with more interesting plants. That's what we try to encourage here, both at the festival and in the gardens. I love it when a teacher brings a school party round and then afterwards some of the children come back bringing their parents. That's my idea of a real success.'

The gardens are open every day except Saturdays from the end of March to the end of October, from 10.30 a.m. to 5.30 p.m. For more details, phone 01539 558328, email publicopenings@holker.co.uk or visit www.holker-hall.co.uk.

Stewartia pseudocamellia Koreana Group

Halesia monticola

A Loderi Group rhododendron

PLANT CHOICES

Lord and Lady Cavendish choose some of their favourites for a woodland garden on acid soil. These include trees and shrubs as well as herbaceous plants and bulbs for planting between them.

1. Any of the *Styracaceae*, which are acid-loving large shrubs or small trees with pure white bell-shaped flowers in late spring or early summer. *Halesia monticola* is a good one to choose, though H. *monticola* var. *vestita*, with considerably larger flowers, is perhaps even better.

2. *Embothrium coccineum*, a large shrub or small evergreen tree from Chile with a profusion of dramatic scarlet flowers in May and June.

3. One of the rhododendrons of the Loderi Group. There is a whole group of Loderi hybrids and nowadays they are more correctly listed under their individual names, such as 'Loderi King George', which is the best known and most spectacular, with pink buds opening to pure white. All make large shrubs or small trees.

4. Eucryphias – any. Mostly sizeable shrubs or small trees, grown for their saucer-shaped and usually white flowers in late summer. Some are evergreen, some deciduous, and some are distinctly hardier than others. The cultivar known as 'Nymansay' is one of the hardiest and most frequently seen.

5. *Oxydendrum arboreum*, a large shrub or small tree from the US, with outstanding autumn colour.

6. Stewartias – any of these camellia relatives with white flowers in late summer and spectacular autumn colour. *S. pseudocamellia* is the most commonly seen and one of the hardiest.

7. Species crocus.

8. *Cardiocrinum giganteum*.

9. Hellebores.

YEWBARROW HOUSE, GRANGE-OVER-SANDS

There are mature gardens, aged over decades or centuries, and there are very recent gardens, still 'under construction'. At Yewbarrow House above Grange-over-Sands, overlooking Morecambe Bay from the steep slopes of Hampsfell, there is a rare example of both co-existing in a single remarkable garden.

The house was built in the mid-nineteenth century and its 4 acres or so of garden are on what Victorian sale particulars described as 'a singularly dry and warm Limestone formation … completely sheltered from the North' with 'a Southern aspect'. When Jonathan Denby, his wife Margaret and their three young children arrived in 1999, however, the house was almost invisible within a jungle of overlarge trees and overgrown shrubs, particularly laurels and hydrangeas. Most of the laurels and hydrangeas were immediately either rooted out or reduced, and the trees ruthlessly thinned. Ever since, as soon as a newly cleared area has become available, it has been redesigned and replanted.

OPPOSITE Looking down from the top of the turreted folly into the Gravel Garden, with its population of tender exotics, including huge cycads and echiums.

BELOW Victorian theatricality between the top of the Italian Terrace Garden and the Gravel Garden, with dahlias on the left and dramatic foliage plants on either side of the border beyond.

Several factors have contributed to the garden's redevelopment. The first is three lively young children, who on this steep site needed safe flat areas in which to play. Hence the flat Sunken Garden, excavated from a rough grass bank on the side of the house from which visitors approach. In part, this area has also been determined by the fact that this is a garden very much designed to be viewed from the windows of the house. (It is hardly surprising that window views are important here, given the enormous non-garden ones out over Morecambe Bay.) Digging out for the Sunken Garden its uphill side uncovered some spectacular limestone 'pavements', clearly too beautiful to be hidden, so the planned lawn became considerably narrower. Then Jonathan's friend Christopher Holliday, garden designer, writer and enthusiast for 'architectural exotics', encouraged him to concentrate on semi-tender and mostly evergreen plants with strong shapes, so that even in winter the area would still be visually strong. Hence the telegraph pole of a palm in the centre of the lawn, the young specimens of Mexican blue palm (*Brahea armata*) in the beds, together with bamboos, euphorbias, grevilleas, strelitzias, agaves, dasylirions and a spectacular stand of lush-leaved, red-flowered *Lobelia tupa*. On a sunny day, with the bay glittering down below,

this area feels more like the south of France than the south of Cumbria.

That feeling is intensified if you leave the Sunken Garden, cross the drive and look up. At once you are confronted by what Jonathan calls the Italian Terrace Garden. This consists of five substantial recently built stone-walled terraces, marching boldly up the hillside. Standard lollipops of *Pittosporum tobira* flank the central path, while smaller balls of *P. tobira* 'Nanum' edge the front of each bed – an idea he cheerfully confesses to having stolen from the promenade at San Remo. The rest of the planting is an equally theatrical and conscious recreation of the most fashionable late-Victorian style. A great admirer of the Victorian garden writer Shirley Hibberd, he has adopted many of his suggestions. So, though in spring each of these beds is massed with tulips, in summer these are replaced by dramatic rows of ginger lilies (*Hedychium* spp.), gladioli, dahlias and cannas.

The same theatrical fizz is to be found throughout the Yewbarrow House garden. At the top of the Italian Terrace Garden, for instance, you go through a door and find yourself in the walled Gravel Garden, of which the back wall is an extravagant turreted folly. Here the exotic planting and the feeling that you are in some fantastic fairytale world, far from Cumbria, reaches a climax. A formal design of gravel-

surfaced (and hence heat-reflecting) raised beds is dominated by several huge specimens of the cycad *Cycas revoluta* and an array of bananas. These are no 'ordinary' bananas (the relatively hardy *Musa basjoo*), but either the rare red-leaved *Ensete ventricosum* 'Maurelii' or the even rarer *E. ventricosum* 'Montbeliardii'. Around them is arranged a collection of smaller tender exotics, all with impressive foliage and relishing life in this sheltered, heat-holding, well-drained, south-facing enclosure. Even *Echium pininana*, *Melianthus major* and *Fascicularia bicolor* are unusual in the north. Such rarities as *Colocasia esculenta*, *Alocasia macrorrhiza* and the unfortunately named but strikingly foliaged globbas (including *G. cathcartii* and *G. andersonii*) are normally seen only in the most sheltered of gardens in the far south-west, yet they flourish in the ground here year-round, with minimal protection if any.

Alongside the Gravel Garden is the formal walled Kitchen Garden, now restored to a traditional design of elaborate formality – and to traditional levels of productivity. On the slope above, a new cutting garden has been established, with, alongside it, for the moment, a mighty polytunnel full of tender vegetables such as peppers and aubergines. By the time this book appears the polytunnel will have been

LEFT The Sunken Garden, with the massive excavated outcrop of limestone pavement on the left. The border at the end contains sun-loving and slightly tender plants such as grevilleas, myrtles and cistus.

ABOVE The tower lookout at the topmost point of the garden. The Denbys call it the Prospect Tower because it offers spectacular views both towards the Lake District fells and out over the bay and into Lancashire.

FOLLOWING PAGES The 'infinity edge' of the hot spring's pool seems almost to merge into the bay beyond.

replaced by a stone-built orangery against the garden's upper wall. The orangery is intended to act as both a vista-stopper at the top of the garden and as a point from which to gain the most spectacular views down over the garden and out across the bay. All these more or less functional areas have been heavily influenced by the fact that the Denbys are the owners of several local hotels. Yewbarrow's organic fruit and vegetables supply the hotels' kitchens, while its cut flowers fill the hotels' rooms.

The main slope is split in two by a dividing hedge running from top to bottom. Jonathan calls it a thicket, since this is no ordinary hedge but

one made of palm trees (a mixture of *Trachycarpus fortunei* and *Chamaerops humilis*). The garden's next *coup de théâtre* is that, on the far side of the thicket, you suddenly change continents. The mood becomes Japanese rather than Mediterranean, as a curving path, edged on either side with rows of *Acer palmatum* var. *dissectum* Dissectum Atropurpureum Group leads up the slope (unmodified on this side by terracing) to a garden in Japanese style. Its surface is completely covered in marble chippings except for two twisted and characterful conifers in Oriental style, one on either side of an equally curving rivulet carrying water down to the unlikely climax of a Japanese hot spring. The spring's heating and pumping apparatus is hidden in a tea house beside it, in front of which there is a traditional moon-viewing platform, while the spring itself comes complete with an underwater ledge on which to rest and look out over the bay. The

Formality and functionality are combined in Yewbarrow's splendid reinstatement of traditional kitchen gardening.

front of the pool has an infinity edge, arranged so that it seems to merge into the bay, as though you could swim right out and off to Lancashire. Part of the point of the hot spring, Jonathan explains with a smile, is that 'It gives the children and their friends a place it's fun to splash about in even well into the chilliest Cumbrian autumn.' That combination of canny practicality and high-spirited enjoyment is entirely typical of this exciting and continually expanding garden and of its endlessly enthusiastic creator.

The garden opens under the National Gardens Scheme and for groups by appointment (telephone 01539 532469 or visit www.yewbarrowhouse.co.uk).

Tithonia rotundifolia 'Torch'

Acca sellowiana (syn. *Feijoa sellowiana*)

Echium pininana

PLANT CHOICES

Jonathan Denby describes some of his favourite plants. Many are on the edges of hardiness and some are beyond them, and all will add drama to a sheltered garden.

1. *Beschorneria yuccoides* looks like a modest agave until it flowers, when it produces a 2-metre spire of bright red tubular flowers. It needs full sun, shelter and maximum drainage.

2. The cultivar name of *Canna* 'Musifolia' means that it has leaves like a banana. It certainly does, and the banana in question is the magnificent deep-purple-leaved *Musa ensete*. *C.* 'Musifolia' can shoot up to an amazing 4 metres in a season, and as it's grown for its leaves it doesn't matter whether or not it manages to produce its smallish red flowers before it's blasted by frost. Give it full sun, rich moist soil and lift and store over winter.

3. The silver fern *Cyathea dealbata* has a slender black stem and a crown of lime-green fronds. It is the most handsome of the more or less hardy tree ferns and, as with *Dicksonia antarctica*, at Yewbarrow the fronds stay fresh and green throughout winter under their overhead canopy of yew trees.

4. I love many dahlias, mainly because they produce so many cutting flowers for so long a season. ('Sylvia' and 'Grenadier' are outstanding in that respect.) It may seem perverse to mention one that has never flowered in my garden and is never likely to, but the beauty of *D. imperialis* is that it thinks it's a tree. It towers to 4 metres in a season, with a thick purple stem and masses of small branches festooned in graceful leaves. It needs the same conditions and treatment as *Canna* 'Musifolia'.

5. I've lost more sleep over *Echium pininana* than over any other plant in the garden. It's on the edge of hardiness here, has to be in the open ground, is too bulky to wrap and only flowers in its third season, so it has to survive two full winters. Then when it flowers it dies and you have to start all over again. But when it does flower it's so spectacular that it's worth all the intervening insomnia. Its inflorescence can be up to 4 metres tall, with hundreds of pale blue flowers – a magnet for bees. If you succeed with this one, try *E. wildpretii*, which is slightly smaller but with gorgeous red flowers.

6. I'm fascinated by the extraordinary flowers of the bird of paradise (*Strelitzia reginae*) and amazed and delighted that we manage to give it the conditions to produce them. The trick is to keep it tightly pot bound in an unheated greenhouse over winter, with no water and no attention – in other words, total neglect, which I seem to be able to manage.

7. The purple-leaved banana *Ensete ventricosum* 'Maurelii' is too tender to overwinter in the ground here. Planted out in May, though, it will make 3 metres by midsummer and its magnificent leaves are tough enough to withstand our seaside winds without shredding.

8. The tender giant which used to be *Ferdinanda eminens* and is now *Podachaenium eminens* was described by William Robinson as 'one of the tallest and noblest' plants and indispensable for subtropical effects. As usual, he was right. It is virtually unknown in English gardens nowadays, but I tracked down a supplier in California and it is now producing its 4-metre stems and enormous leaves for us here.

PEAR TREE COTTAGE, BURTON-IN-KENDAL

At Pear Tree Cottage, tucked away in a maze of lanes outside the village of Burton-in-Kendal, Linda Greening and her husband Alec have successfully solved two problems which plague many keen gardeners: how to keep a garden of modest size interesting all season and how to incorporate lots of individual 'specials' but avoid 'spottiness'.

Linda's solution to the first problem has been to design each border so that it doesn't reach a single climax but produces a succession of flowers from spring through to autumn. To solve the second she has used what she describes as 'signature plants and signature colours' to tie the garden together. One such signature plant is *Verbascum chaixii* 'Album', 'an indispensable self-seeder, and what's more it doesn't flop'. Her signature colours are mostly dark reds and 'the mauvey-lilac end of the spectrum'; flowers in those tones pop up throughout the garden.

This sophisticated cottage garden is, then, the result of much careful thought and discriminating planting. And it has been achieved with remarkable speed. Alec and Linda only bought the cottage in 1997 and when they arrived there was very little garden: just, as Linda puts it, 'bits around the edge', and even those were badly overgrown – so overgrown that 'at first we didn't even know that the handsome limestone steps beside the rockery were there'. There were other problems, too, less easily solved. Although the soil here is mostly 'a reasonable loam, slightly the alkaline side of neutral', and therefore suitable for a wide range of plants, the garden is in 'a bit of a frost pocket' and, because it is tucked into the hillside, with woods and the road above it, 'very wet. All the run-off from the road pours down into it.' There were also regular invasions by rabbits and deer, so the garden had to be fenced against both.

Doing that went against the Greenings' instincts, because generally this is a garden where wildlife is encouraged to come in. It has to its credit over fifty species of birds, the first recorded local examples of several rare moths, and a pond well stocked with frogs, newts and dragonflies. And the fact that it is very much a country

Viewed from across the blue and white border below the pergola, the gate into the lane seems almost submerged in flowers and foliage.

garden has had a considerable effect on its style. Linda believes, 'You have to try to make a garden suit the environment around it,' so that means that certain plants and certain colours don't 'fit' here: 'I think cannas are wonderful – but not next to a field.' And she doesn't think hot or 'hard' colours work against the backdrop of grey stone and green grass, so the colours she chooses tend to be softer, if often also rich. Shapes tend to be softer, too – 'I can't be doing with straight lines!' All the beds on this sloping site have flowing curves, which make them seem to emerge naturally from the landscape and merge unobtrusively into it. Even the way she grows her plants is influenced by the garden's situation. 'I try to grow things in a natural way, as they'd grow in their natural environment. For example, I like to grow clematis through shrubs or up trees, rather than on supports.'

As you enter the garden, the bed below the pergola attached to the cottage has blues and whites as its predominant colours: 'deeper tones in spring, lighter ones in summer', Linda explains. These are set off, however, by her favourite colours: scattered pinks, magentas and deep reds such as *Knautia macedonica*, *Astrantia major* 'Claret'

ABOVE The border below the pergola, full of Linda's favourite blues and whites.

RIGHT Looking up from the pond and the densely planted bed above it to the cottage. It is hard to believe that all this is only a few years old.

and *Veronicastrum virginicum* 'Apollo'. It is typical of Linda's thoughtful planting that despite its height the veronicastrum is used in the middle of the border, not at the back, 'to add definition without too much bulk'.

Around the corner, along the boundary with the road, the border begins with a raised stone-walled section. This was Alec's idea and creation. Though Linda is clearly in charge of the planting, she says, 'We do have joint ideas, and Alec is particularly good at ones involving structures.' This long border contains masses of Linda's signature mauves and purples, from early tulips such as 'Queen of Night', through irises and alliums, to penstemons such as 'Raven', aquilegias such as 'William Guinness' and polemoniums such as 'Sonia's Bluebell'. These are all given added impact by the contrasting whites, creams and creamy yellows of *Sisyrinchium striatum* 'Variegatum', *Hydrangea* 'Annabelle' and more of that 'indispensable self-seeder' *Verbascum chaixii* 'Album'.

The border on the far side of the garden is 'meant to be seen from the house'. As a result, it contains bigger shrubs and has a 'bigger' colour scheme, too, in red and gold. The main red-foliaged shrubs are *Physocarpus opulifolius* 'Diabolo', *Sambucus nigra* 'Black Lace', and *Berberis* 'Rose Glow' and *B*. 'Harlequin', while occasional red 'highlights' are added by *Sorbaria sorbifolia*. Linda particularly relishes the way the solid foliage of the physocarpus and the ferny leaves of the sorbaria bring out the best in each other. Yellows and golds here are supplied by *Choisya ternata* 'Sundance', *Berberis thunbergii* 'Aurea' and yellow-leaved fuchsias such as 'Empress of Prussia'.

Below that border is a wonderfully natural-looking pond – though in fact Alec created it only a few years ago. It and its neighbouring boggy area are densely planted with intermingling primulas, irises, astilbes and Alec's beloved ferns. The old apple tree on the edge of the bog garden is swathed in not just one plant but three or four, including a spectacular example of the rose 'Rambling Rector'.

A single plant in this area summed up for me the beauty of this garden and the skill of its gardener. It is not only unusual and beautiful but has been persuaded to fulfil two quite separate functions. That plant is the Japanese shrub *Stephanandra tanakae*. Planted at the end of the red and gold border, its tall, arching habit and cream-into-pink panicles of flowers combine beautifully there with the rounded mass of red-foliaged *Cotinus* 'Grace' and the bold glaucous leaves and upright growth of the plume poppy *Macleaya cordata*.

Linda and Alec's spruce and productive vegetable garden.

Come down the slope, though, walk to the far side of the pond, look back up, and it has become part of the pond planting. In this situation, its arching stems tone perfectly with the massive rounded boulder which forms the capstone at the top of the little cascade. That really is maximizing your space.

The garden opens under the National Gardens Scheme and for small groups by appointment between June and August (telephone 01524 781624 or visit www.peartreecottagecumbria.co.uk). Linda has a permanent plant stall by the roadside, from which 50 per cent of the proceeds go to Unicef or Save the Children.

Looking out from the densely planted pergola by the cottage to the equally densely planted garden beyond. The rose on the pillar is 'Compassion' and that on the trellis on the right the Rambler 'Goldfinch'. The mauve-purple flower top left is *Nemesia* 'Confetti', trailing down from a hanging basket.

Rosa 'Crown Princess Margareta' (syn. 'Auswinter')

Amelanchier lamarckii

Mahonia japonica

PLANT CHOICES

Linda Greening's selection concentrates on plants with a usefully long period of performance.

1. *Stipa gigantea* looks good for months and provides lightness, movement and height without weight. It likes full sun.
2. *Stephanandra tanakae* is a shrub with a graceful habit, beautiful autumn colour and lovely brown stems in winter. It looks good throughout the year. It withstands all pests, is very hardy and seems indifferent to soil or situation.
3. *Amelanchier lamarckii* is lovely in spring with its masses of white flowers and lovely in autumn with wonderful leaf colour. Ours hasn't read the book – it's supposed to like acid soil but though our soil is on the alkaline side of neutral it still thrives.
4. *Osmunda regalis* is such an elegant fern from the time its new croziers unfurl in the spring until it's cut down by autumn frosts. The forms 'Cristata' and 'Purpurascens' offer intriguing variations for fern fans.
5. *Geranium palmatum* is evergreen, is bigger than most other geranium species, has lovely foliage and flowers all summer. Given a warm sheltered spot it copes with quite heavy frosts.
6. *Tiarella polyphylla* is a real sweetie, a dainty and well-behaved ground-cover plant under trees or shrubs, with lovely leaf markings and a long flowering period. It likes shade, is unfussy about soil and self-sows gently but is never a nuisance.
7. *Cotinus* 'Grace' is a wonderful foliage plant throughout the season and in autumn it becomes breathtaking. Plant it where the light can shine through the leaves – which are almost translucent, like stained glass – and you're in heaven.
8. *Knautia macedonica* blooms its socks off all summer and into autumn, and the bees love its dusky pincushion flowers, which make a good counterpoint to softer pastel shades. It likes full sun but doesn't seem to be fussy about soil.
9. *Astrantia major* 'Roma' has a really long season and all the virtues of all the other astrantias, but flowers in a lovely shade of pink. It likes decent soil in sun or part shade.
10. *Rosa* 'Crown Princess Margareta' (aka *R.* 'Auswinter') is disease resistant, has a long flowering season, and has scented and ruffled double flowers of a wonderful rich apricot colour. It can be grown as either a shrub or a short climber.
11. *Mahonia japonica* always offers its lovely glossy evergreen leaves and is covered in fragrant yellow flowers in winter, just when you need something to cheer you up. It prefers full or partial shade but copes with sun if the soil is reasonably moist.
12. *Thalictrum rochebruneanum* may not have as long a season of interest as my other choices but it's so gorgeous, so light and airy as it floats above almost all other herbaceous plants that I just had to include it.

Holme Crag, Witherslack

To visit the garden Jack Watson spent thirty years creating at Holme Crag, Witherslack, high in the hills above Morecambe Bay in the far south of Cumbria, is to step back in time. In many ways Holme Crag belongs to an earlier and simpler age, when country gardening was done on a shoestring out of sheer love, with plants all grown from seed and structures improvised by the gardener. There are also ways, though, in which it reflects contemporary interests, for it is as much a piece of 'cultivated ecology' as a conventional garden. Jack is interested not just in cultivated plants but in encouraging wild plants, birds, animals and insects to adopt his 4-acre site.

When Jack and his late wife first came here, virtually everything was swathed in a dense blanket of brambles, bracken and gorse. What is now the central broad lawn leading down to the garden's central large pond was an almost impenetrable jungle, with brambles arching over from either side. Nowadays, visitors' eyes are caught by (and their feet guided across) a dozen or more beautiful rocky outcrops. In the beginning, though, just one of those outcrops was visible; the others were only discovered when they started hacking back the undergrowth. Over time, the brambles were laboriously removed by hand, while Jack found that if he cut down gorse to below ground level, it didn't regenerate. For areas infested with bracken or other obstinate 'herbaceous' weeds, he developed a method of covering them with black plastic or polythene, edging them with rough windfall timber and filling to the top of the timber with compost. For the following two years, these areas were nursery beds. When compost, timber and plastic were finally removed, there was virtually weed-free soil beneath.

However, plants which in other gardens would be weeds (brambles and gorse among them) Jack has sometimes permitted and even encouraged as a food source for wildlife. Similarly, some wild grassy areas are not cut until summer's end, either because birds such as warblers feed off the grasses' seedheads or because the area contains interesting wild flowers. For example, below the central pond is a stretch once cropped by sheep to a close turf but for many

Astilbes and hostas beside the pool and white and red water lilies within it.

Spring at Holme Crag brings an explosion of colour from huge expanses of Candelabra primulas. These self-hybridize and self-sow to produce an ever-increasing range of colours and quantity of flowers.

with no guarantees,' says Jack, 'so it didn't do badly.' A few years ago, it finally began to leak, and so he replaced the pond with a slightly smaller butyl-lined one, with a second miniature pondlet alongside for the moorhens that nest in the irises round its edge. Characteristically this was not an aesthetic decision so much as a practical one. Since pond liner comes in square pieces, a single pond of the original shape (longer than wide, with a bulge to one side) would have involved expensive waste; two smaller squarer ponds made better economic sense. First, though, Jack laboriously lifted the plants in and around the original pond and saved them for re-use. Edging plants include bamboos, sedges, grasses, astilbes, hostas and Candelabra primulas, while water inhabitants include water lilies, water hawthorn (*Aponogeton distachyos*) and the showy blue-flowered pickerel weed (*Pontederia cordata*). Even the pond mud was carefully conserved and re-used, for the sake of the creatures whose home it is.

Although this is not a garden which aims at display, plants are as sensitively encouraged as birds, animals and insects. Their positioning may be determined by where they will do best rather than by where they will make the biggest show, but as a result the garden's 'season' hardly ever ends. Ask Jack when is the best time to visit and he simply says, 'Come when you like. There's always something to see.' And indeed there is, for in a laid-back way Jack is a considerable plantsman. You will find here many trees which are unusual in being grown from seed or cuttings, including a 40-foot-high *Robinia pseudoacacia*. Among herbaceous plants are oddities such as several unusual species of *Eupatorium*, grown for both their bold beauty and their attractiveness to insects and butterflies; fine flourishing clumps of several species of *Roscoea*; and swathes of the Welsh poppy (*Meconopsis cambrica*) in its unusual double form, in three different shades – yellow, orange and the rare red. Quieter beauties include more than forty unusual varieties of fern and some equally unusual ivies running happily up the trunks of conifers.

years now untouched by either sheep or sprays; as a result, many rare wild flowers have re-emerged, much to the fascination of local botanists. Trees and shrubs such as cotoneaster and sorbus are there not only because they look good and thrive in this semi-moorland setting but also because their berries provide food for birds. The (unfenced) garden's larger animal inhabitants have included a resident though seldom seen badger, deer, hares, rabbits, stoats, weasels and a vixen, who became so accustomed to Jack that she stayed on the lawn with her cubs even when she knew he was close by. In addition there have sometimes been over thirty different species of bird in the garden in a season, and it can claim three species of dragonfly and five of damselfly.

The large pond is a hotbed of bird and insect activity. It looks entirely natural but is all Jack's own work – twice over. Nearly thirty years ago he dug it out and lined it with black polythene. 'It came

There is a path – just – meandering through this poolside planting.

Holme Crag's 4 acres are Jack's single-handed creation. Each year he has always grown hundreds of plants from seed and cuttings. Each year he has planted, pruned, weeded, lifted, divided. He has recycled bamboo and sedge as path surfacing, and tree prunings as railings beside paths; and he has always still somehow found time to put out 9 pounds of bird food every week. He has also always had the garden open, all day every day, right through the year. The amazing thing, though, is that Jack was a sixty-year-old retired farmer when he first came here and when I visited in 2005 he was eighty-nine.

Sadly, in 2006 Jack had to bow to advancing years and Holme Crag has now been sold. But the new owners are, unsurprisingly, in love with the garden and it seems likely that it will still be open to the public, at least for a day or two each year.

Consult the Yellow Book to see if Holme Crag is still opening under the National Gardens Scheme.

Halecat, Witherslack

Mrs Fortune Stanley and her late husband, Michael, came to Halecat, at the head of a valley in the quiet rural southern foothills of the Lake District, just after the Second World War. The solid mid-nineteenth-century limestone house of unostentatious dignity enjoys a site with splendid and extensive views southwards as far as the distant Forest of Bowland. However, the 1½ acres of garden were then boldly designed but very bare. In Mrs Stanley's phrase, it was simply 'a square upon a square': the upper square was the imposing lawn just below the level of the house, and it was surrounded by a lower and larger square. Everywhere there were handsome but unadorned stone retaining walls, while a more fundamental problem was the poor, stony, highly alkaline soil.

Many might have been daunted by such circumstances, but Mrs Stanley is from a family which for generations has produced dedicated and knowledgeable gardeners, including her sister, Faith Raven of Docwra's Manor and Ardtornish, and her mother, who had most influence on the way the garden at Halecat developed. Indeed, one border in the lower garden, which she helped to design, is in her honour called Mrs Smith's Border. Guided by her mother and her own instincts, Mrs Stanley's governing intention was as much as possible to soften, and distract attention from, the garden's geometrical lines and bare stone walls.

One method she used to distract was the addition of architectural eye-catchers. These were provided in the early 1960s by Francis Johnson, a modern architect in a Classical style. He introduced a fine broad flight of steps to link the terrace to the upper lawn and two pairs of obelisks, one pair sited on either side of the top of those steps and the other on either side of the main path at the point at which the upper garden begins to fall down towards the lower. For the lowest and most distant corner of the lower garden he designed a delicious 'Gothic' summerhouse, complete with fan-vaulted ceiling and stained-glass panels as centrepieces in its pointed windows. (It now boasts its own Grade II listing.)

A second method of distraction was the use of what might be described as horticultural eye-catchers: plants designed to catch the

OPPOSITE *Rosa* 'Fritz Nobilis' running down either side of the steps, designed by Francis Johnson, which lead from the terrace to the main lawn.

BELOW Variegated pollarded poplars are underplanted with the geraniums *G. × magnificum*, *G. endressii* and *G.e.* 'Wargrave's Pink'.

FOLLOWING PAGES Sections of the long border along the edge of the upper lawn.

LEFT The fine latticing and stained glass of the 'Gothick' windows of the summerhouse.

RIGHT Francis Johnson's summerhouse or gazebo.

eye and disguise the garden's basic four-square-ness, such as specimens of variegated poplar, tightly pruned to make narrow vertical columns at regular intervals around the lawn. Other variegated or dramatically coloured trees and shrubs form the backbone planting throughout the garden. For example, the length and straightness of a long double border in the lower garden below the side of the house have been cunningly disguised by the division of the border into three 'semi-rooms' and by the bold planting of facing pairs of vividly coloured shrubs, including *Cotinus coggygria* 'Royal Purple', *Pyrus salicifolia*, golden philadelphus (*P. coronarius* 'Aureus'), *Berberis thunbergii* f. *atropurpurea* and golden ribes (*R. odoratum*). These geometrical plantings are softened by lushly abundant under- and interplanting, in which contrasts of colour are more important than continuity of colour, and the colour and form of foliage are quite as important as flower colour.

Mrs Smith's Border, on the other hand, running down the slope which links lawn with lower garden, was designed originally to consist mostly of pinks, purples, greys and blue-greys. The glaucous foliage of a fine specimen of *Paeonia mlokosewitschii* with a flanking pair of *Berberis thunbergii* f. *atropurpurea* 'Atropurpurea Nana' is a particularly striking combination. Nowadays, however, though those colours still predominate, other colours have been allowed gently to infiltrate. Throughout, the planting is relaxed, unfussy, almost cottagey. There is room both for individual specimens of special small treasures and for large blocks of plants that might be considered thugs, such as *Macleaya cordata*, which has been permitted to make a solid block, acting as a full stop at the bottom of the border.

During the 1990s, though, relaxation began to go too far. Thugs were starting to demonstrate their thuggishness, weaker and smaller plants were being lost and serious weeds were beginning to infiltrate. So the decision was taken to appoint a new head gardener who would revive the garden. Matthew Bardgett trained at Montacute, and worked first at Mottisfont and then at the Cumbrian National Trust gardens at Hill Top and Townend. At Mottisfont he learnt the importance of 'precise edges and precise pruning', while Hill Top and Townend made him sympathetic to abundant planting in a cottage-garden style. These influences made him the perfect choice to revivify a garden which combines them.

And 'revivify', he insists, is the appropriate word. 'I'm fine-tuning, that's all. Tinkering, not redesigning.' He is grateful, though, that Mrs Stanley is perfectly happy for the garden to change. An example can be seen at the beginning of the double border, where graceful fountains of *Stipa gigantea* now contrast beautifully with the solid blocks of *Cotinus coggygria* 'Royal Purple' behind them. Grasses generally, indeed, are increasingly being introduced, to add lightness and airiness to a garden of rather solid foliage. And in the big border along the edge of the lawn a much wider range of flower colour is being developed. The blue which had become too predominant has now been varied by the introduction of lobelias and day lilies, globe flowers (*Trollius*) and asters.

Matthew's summary of what he is trying to do would surely meet with Mrs Stanley's agreement even if she probably wouldn't put it in quite the same way: 'I'm just trying to get everything to look as near damn beautiful as I can.' After all, that's what she's been trying, very successfully, to do here for almost sixty years.

The garden opens under the National Gardens Scheme and is open all year to individuals. Entry is free of charge, though donations to an honesty box are invited. Visits by larger groups can be arranged by writing to Matthew Bardgett, Halecat, Witherslack, Grange-over-Sands, Cumbria LA11 6RT. A small nursery attached to the garden, stocking many of the plants to be found in it, is open throughout the March–October season (www.halecat.co.uk, telephone 01539 552536).

LEVENS HALL

Even the most casual visitor tends to know that the garden at Levens Hall in the far south of Cumbria is an almost unique survivor from the late seventeenth century. Its survival, however, was an inspired accident. For several generations the house was a sort of glorified holiday home, a relatively minor property owned by a family with several other larger houses in more fashionable areas, which meant that they only occasionally visited Levens. When it was not used like that it was used as a sort of 'dower house' for elderly relatives. As a result its gardens were not changed by each succeeding generation to the latest fashionable style, as they would have been had it been the family's main house. By the time its owners were again living full-time at Levens, the preservation of picturesque relics from the past had itself become the latest fashion, so change for change's sake was no longer a desirable option.

It therefore still retains much of its original layout of hedged compartments in the formal style fashionable in the seventeenth century – and in particular the compartment containing its parterre and its famous accompanying topiary shapes. Standing in the middle of that bizarre company of surreal green giants, visitors often feel as though they have stepped back in time. 'When they first come in through the little entrance doorway and find themselves straight-away in the middle of the topiary,' says Chris Crowder, Levens Hall's head gardener for the past twenty years, 'you can see that they're deeply impressed and sometimes really inspired.'

As far as the topiary is concerned, the Levens gardeners are essentially maintenance men. Living with the garden every day, Chris tends to notice more than the topiary 'the weeds, the things we haven't got right. And I remember that it's two months' hard work over autumn and winter to get it and the hedges all clipped.' Here his job is one of preserving rather than creating; it is the part of the garden where, inevitably, he has been least able to make his personal mark. However, he says, 'We have started about thirty new pieces, which we'll be shaping in the years to come.'

The visitors' feeling of 'stepping back in time' when they view the topiary shapes and the parterre which acts as their setting is to an extent an illusion. Though the topiary garden still has the same 'bones', the plants originally used to infill the parterre would have

OPPOSITE 'White Triumphator' tulips fill this section of the ancient parterre.

ABOVE Looking from the parterre to the end of Beaumont's house, built for him in 1701. The house is always occupied by the head gardener; Chris Crowder is only the tenth in 300 years. The sundial, of course, is an hour out in British Summer Time.

FOLLOWING PAGES Looking towards the vegetable borders and the hall beyond through late-season plantings of cannas (*Canna indica* 'Purpurea') and dahlias ('Bishop of Llandaff').

been much less colourful and would have had a far shorter season than the eye-catching cultivars used today. Chris points out, 'Had we used the original plants, only a fraction of our visitors would have known what we were doing or why, or would have enjoyed the result.' Instead, nowadays there are spectacular displays of spring and summer bedding. Some of the plants used change from year to year but there is also a stock company of reliable regulars, such as 'White Triumphator' and 'Queen of Night' tulips in spring and *Verbena rigida* and yellow antirrhinums in summer. Even though the infill plants are modern, the overwhelming visual effect of the giant, closely clipped pieces of topiary rising out of a sea of flowers is still very much the same – an effect which has been the keynote of the garden for over three hundred years.

'Visual effect' and hence 'huge impact', both deriving from the combination of the formal and the theatrical, are the garden's core strengths. In Chris's words, 'It's almost as though this part of the garden was set up as a series of photo-opportunities, centuries before there were cameras to take advantage of them.' Modern developments elsewhere in the garden have followed and intensified that idea by adding more and more dramatic episodes. That approach

OPPOSITE Part of the Levens parterre, infilled in summer with *Antirrhinum majus* 'Liberty Classic Yellow' in the foreground and far distance, a blue form of *Aegeratum leillanii* to the left, and *Verbena rigida* in the middle distance.

ABOVE 'White Triumphator' tulips in the parterre.

can best be seen in the garden's long and deep double borders. These include the pastel borders, the red and purple borders and, more surprisingly, the vegetable borders. The latter often come in for particularly fervent praise in the Levens Hall visitors book, where the most common description of them is 'unusual and effective'. Which indeed they are, because the plants in them are used for decorative and dramatic effect, in the style of a herbaceous border, rather than being planted in rows as they would be in a traditional kitchen garden.

All these double borders are planned on the boldest possible lines, as they have to be in a garden of this scale. A relatively restricted palette of plants is employed because, Chris says, 'We use mostly the plants which years of experience have taught us really work.'

These plants occur over and over again, in big repeated blocks. The blocks are repeated on either side of the central path too, giving the viewer a visual 'double whammy'. As with the parterre and its topiary pieces, the cumulative effect is powerfully dramatic.

This large garden was once maintained by a dozen or more gardeners. Now there are five, which, with modern machinery, is, says its perfectionist head gardener, 'just enough for us to keep on top of it'. In the past, gardeners stayed in one garden for decades, sometimes for their whole lives; at least one head gardener worked at Levens for seventy years. Nowadays, like everyone else, gardeners tend to move every few years in search of promotion. By staying for twenty years Chris is one of the few to buck that trend. 'And', he says, 'I shall probably be here for another twenty, until I retire.'

Levens Hall and Gardens are open Sundays to Thursdays from 12 April to 13 October, from 10.00 a.m. to 5.00 p.m. For more information, telephone 01539 560321, email houseopening@levenshall.co.uk or visit www.levenshall.co.uk.

ABOVE Looking from the hot 'red' borders out to the ha-ha and the field beyond.

RIGHT, ABOVE The orchard has been 'formalized' with squares of long grass at the base of each tree and each square planted with bulbs. Here the bulbs are 'Apeldoorn' tulips.

RIGHT, BELOW The Rose Garden, filled with David Austin's English roses.

Another view of the Rose Garden and David Austin's English roses.

Tulipa 'Queen of Night'

Cleome spinosa

Tulipa 'White Triumphator'

PLANT CHOICES

Head gardener Chris Crowder discusses some of his favourite flowers and vegetables.

1. My favourite summer bedding plants are *Argyranthemum foeniculare*, which has good silvery foliage and endless little white daisies from the time you put it in the ground until the first frosts in October; *Verbena rigida* (also known as *V. venosa*), which flowers late but goes on for a long time, while its lavender haze of flowers gives just the right old-fashioned look for this garden; and *Antirrhinum majus* 'Liberty Classic Yellow', which is a good performer and a classic enough colour to look old-fashioned even if it isn't – and one which combines perfectly with the colour of the verbena. In spring my favourites are double 'Medicis' daisies and the tulips 'White Triumphator' and 'Queen of Night'.

2. My favourite shrubs for mixed borders are the silver willow (*Salix alba* var. *sericea*), which looks like a fountain when pollarded, and *Cornus alba* 'Aurea', which is a good doer with nice golden-yellow foliage – and it doesn't burn out in sun. It combines well with my other favourite, the purple vine *Vitis vinifera* 'Purpurea'.

3. My favourite decorative vegetables are asparagus – the feathery foliage of which we use as an informal hedge – and the purple-podded Italian pole bean 'Viola de Cornetto'. That's good for the pot as well as in the border, by the way, though sadly the beans turn green when boiled.

4. My favourite 'filler' plant, for wherever there's a hole in a border, is *Cleome spinosa*. It's amazing the way something which looks so delicate grows so quickly to become so big. And it's absolutely stormproof – it always looks good whatever the weather.

Sizergh Castle

The National Trust in Cumbria is so identified with the vast tracts of the Lake District landscape it owns that its houses and even more its gardens here sometimes tend to get rather passed over. The garden at Sizergh Castle near Levens is an example: not enough people visit it, and too many of those who do walk through it just because they have to on their way to the castle.

New young head gardener John Hawley hopes that will not be the case for much longer, especially as he has plans to develop it. As far as he's concerned, Sizergh is an ideal garden at which to be head gardener: because the garden mostly dates back only to the 1920s and planting records for it are very incomplete, he has more room for manoeuvre and experiment than he would in a garden tied to a specific period or to specific plants.

The garden falls into two very different main sections. In the first – to your front and right, if you stand with your back to the castle – small formal terraces descend to a semicircular 'promontory' above a splendid pool, which has a flourishing population of ancient carp and is so large that it comes complete with its own island. It used to have a miniature echo in the shape of a tiny pond in the centre of the promontory, with its own miniature fountain, but these have long since been turned into a circular flowerbed with the plume-like foliage of a yucca standing in for the vanished fountain.

The front edge of the top terrace is protected by an ancient yew hedge, which decades ago had a 'battlemented' top in imitation of the tower behind it. That was too labour intensive to restore but, instead of leaving the hedge as a simple box shape, John has treated it as a 'cloud hedge' by making improvised undulations in its sides when he clips it in August. 'It was an experiment,' he says, 'and I waited a bit nervously to see how the public responded. But the comments have all been favourable, so I might take the idea further.'

To the right of the terraces are two subordinate but connected areas. The first is the Dutch Garden, a long narrow compartment which in old photographs taken in late summer looks very imposing, with a central flagged path, formal stone steps and

One of Sizergh's great sights is, on a still day, the castle mirrored in the pool.

dahlia-filled beds running its full length on either side. During the Second World War, though, that was all lost (including, sadly, the stonework) when it was grassed and used as a field. The Trust redesigned it in the 1980s with a suitably formal avenue of *Prunus* 'Shirotae' running down its centre. That should eventually join both across its width and down its length, so that it forms a solid tunnel of blossom every spring. The rest of the garden is still just grass. There are plans to try to reinstate the side beds, though that will not be easy as the trees make more and more shade.

Above and beyond the Dutch Garden is the South Garden, one of two possible entrance points to the garden as a whole. At the moment this is an odd mixture, with a central avenue of young yews leading to a formal seat at the far end and informal island beds on either side of the yews, each planted with a

combination of shrubs and ground-covering herbaceous plants. Higher up still is a south-facing fruit wall, an eighteenth-century survivor which is now home to climbers such as *Solanum crispum*. At its foot a narrow herbaceous border gets its focus from masses of penstemons and repeated clumps of the bold foliage of *Acanthus spinosissimus*.

The second major section of the garden, to the left and below as you stand in front of the castle, is a 1920s rockery, an acre or so in size, the largest limestone garden of that sort which the Trust owns. Natural though it looks, it is in fact artificial, having been built by Hayes of Ambleside with rock from the fells above (which was legal then but certainly would not be now). The rockery has become a considerable period feature in its own right, since it contains much of its original planting. It is so big that there are specimens of every possible size, from hefty trees,

such as unusual conifers and Japanese maples (wonderful in spring and autumn), through herbaceous plants such as geraniums, down to small bulbs and alpines. There are also many moisture-loving plants beside the stream winding through it, including representatives of Sizergh's four National Collections of ferns. It has a long and colourful flowering season, but John comments, 'What struck me most about it when I first saw it was that I'd never in my life seen so many different shades of green.'

Beyond those two main areas the garden contains a number of smaller attractions. These include a wildflower meadow on a bank by the pool (containing at least six different native orchid species); a fine orchard made out of what was once the kitchen garden; a second and much larger herbaceous border (redesigned about twenty years ago to focus on reds, purples and mauves, and with a secondary emphasis on good foliage); a new wetland area

The castle on its promontory, seen from the Dutch Garden below, with the young avenue of *Prunus* 'Shirotae' in full bloom.

(with kingfishers as frequent visitors); and a vegetable and cutting garden which John has recently designed.

The whole gardened area amounts to about 18 acres and John and his equally youthful assistant are the only permanent staff. Maintaining and developing such a large area with such minimal manning levels poses a formidable challenge – but John clearly relishes facing it. This is a garden that is a pleasure to visit now, and its evolution will be fascinating to observe in the years to come.

The garden is open Sundays to Thursdays from the end of March to the end of October, from 11.00 to 5.00 p.m. (it is closed Fridays and Saturdays). For more information, telephone the estate office on 01539 560951.

MUNCASTER CASTLE, RAVENGLASS

The gardens at Muncaster Castle are big and spectacular and form part of an even bigger and more spectacular landscape. Their 77 undulating acres, though only a mile or two inland from the coast, are at the beginning of that sudden mighty upheaval, the Eskdale fells, glimpses of which add drama to almost every vista in what is already a dramatic garden.

The garden's situation and climate make it ideal for growing trees and shrubs from the Himalayas and well suited to growing many from South America and New Zealand, such as nothofagus and eucryphia. Its proximity to the Irish Sea means that its climate is moist but its winters are relatively mild, while its hilliness provides excellent drainage. And, like so much of the Lake District, it has acid soil, perfect for such mostly lime-hating plants.

Above all, these factors make it suited to rhododendrons. The long and winding road from the entrance down to the castle is flanked on either side by tiers of rhododendrons and azaleas, which make an overwhelming display for most of the spring and early summer. Other members of the genus play a predominant – but, skilfully, not an overwhelming – part in the rest of the garden: Muncaster has huge collections both of hybrids and, particularly, species. Indeed, Patrick Gordon-Duff-Pennington, whose wife, Phyllida, is the present owner, proudly points out that between the world wars the garden was internationally famous for having the most comprehensive collection of species in Europe.

Though rhododendrons now form its backbone, in fact the garden predates the introduction of most rhododendrons to Europe. In the late eighteenth century the 1st Lord Muncaster planted thousands of hardwoods, such as oak, beech and chestnut, to form large shelter belts, without which gardening here would be almost impossible because of the wind – particularly the savage north-easterly known as the Birker Blow, which is this garden's main enemy.

A dense and colourful planting of azaleas around the summerhouse on the terrace, including yellow *Rhododendron luteum*, pink *R*. 'Hinomayo' and red *R*. 'Hinode-giri'.

Though many of Lord Muncaster's original trees survive, 'They're getting towards the end of their lives,' Patrick explains, 'and they're going to cause us expensive trouble soon.' In the great storm of January 2005, the garden lost several hundred trees, including a mature *Nothofagus betuloides*. Another essential early addition to the garden, and still one of its most eye-catching features, was the long deck-like grassed terrace, designed as a viewing platform from which to appreciate the panorama of the high fells rising in the distance.

The first Himalayan rhododendron species and their hybrids were being planted around the terrace and throughout the garden in the middle of the nineteenth century, and many of these are now enormous. They include a row of huge specimens of 'Broughtonii', a hybrid with what Patrick describes as 'offensive bluish-red flowers' on the edge of the valley between the castle and the stables. 'I hate them!' he says. 'They remind me of my mother-in-law's earrings. She was a very beautiful woman and I was fond of her but for earrings she wore psychedelic tiddlywinks from Woolworths.' However, it was Phyllida Gordon-Duff-Pennington's grandfather, Sir John Ramsden, who was responsible for planting most of Muncaster's rhododendrons. Between the two world wars he helped finance expeditions by planthunters such as George Sherriff and Frank Kingdon-Ward, which is why Muncaster has such a comprehensive collection of their introductions. Sir John was also keen on hybrids, and created many of his own. Most of them were named after members of his family, such as the fine, scented, white, late-flowering 'Joan Ramsden', named after his wife. Patrick

remembers that where 'your' variety got planted depended on how well or badly you behaved. 'The naughtier you were, the further out you were put.'

From Sir John's death in 1958 until the Gordon-Duff-Penningtons arrived in 1982 there was little new planting and a lack of maintenance. At first, 'There was an enormous amount to do. The terrace, for example, was originally 24 feet wide but had shrunk substantially because shrubs had got out of control.' Despite diminished resources compared to those available in the great days between the wars, reclamation has been continuous ever since (helped by grants from English Heritage and the Millennium Commission). Equally continuous has been exciting new planting. 'I wasn't trained in horticulture,' explained Patrick, 'but when Phyllida and I were first married I looked

after sheep in the mornings and learnt from Sir John in the afternoon. He was in a wheelchair by then but still shouting orders.' Later David Davidian of the Edinburgh Botanic Garden extended Patrick's knowledge and in 1970 he travelled to Nepal to see plants in their natural habitat. In the 1990s he encouraged the introduction of many new species, grown from seed collected by Alan Clark in Nepal, China and Tibet. These were planted in newly cleared areas above the drive, now known as the Sino-Himalayan Garden. Many have not yet

Each year, this grove of Muncaster hybrids is one of the garden's great sights. Patrick sums up its appeal by telling the story of how some years ago he saw a little girl run into the middle of it and then turn to call to her mother, who was coming along behind, 'Mummy, it's a dream of flowers.'

reached flowering size but always some rarity somewhere is performing for the first time, such as the Vietnamese *R. leptocladon*, which has strange lime-green flowers 'about which everyone's been very excited'. Not that all the new plantings are rhododendrons. The aim here is to try to imitate a natural 'mixed planting'. So acers, sorbus, magnolias, cotoneasters and hydrangeas intermingle with the rhododendrons and are underplanted with drifts of bulbs and herbaceous species.

A garden like this is a long-term venture. Its timescale is not so much years or decades as centuries. There are trees here planted two centuries ago which are coming to the ends of their lives and others planted ten years ago which will take another century or more to mature. That is why Patrick Gordon-Duff-Pennington is so keen to emphasize the importance of everyone – family, gardeners and visitors – feeling actively involved in ensuring that it continues to flourish.

PREVIOUS PAGES The castle with the valley plunging away below and the Eskdale fells beginning to rise in the distance.

ABOVE Even less-than-major paths are dense with rhododendrons and drifts of primulas.

Except during January, the garden is open daily, from 10.30 a.m. to 6.00 p.m. It is also open from dusk until 9.00 p.m., illuminated by lights, on Saturdays and Sundays from early February until the end of March. If you want to explore the 77 acres really fully, you can stay overnight in bed and breakfast accommodation in the Coachman's Quarters. The castle is open Sunday to Friday, from 12 February to 5 November, 12 noon to 5.00 p.m and on Bank Holiday Saturdays. For more information, telephone 01229 717614, email info@muncaster.co.uk or visit www.muncaster.co.uk.

Rhododendron spinuliferum

Eucryphia cordifolia

Populus tremula

PLANT CHOICES

Patrick Gordon-Duff-Pennington chooses a few favourites from among Muncaster's hundreds of rhododendrons – and a few non-rhododendrons as well.

1. *Rhododendron beanianum*, with waxy red flowers and dark brown indumentum, is a fine plant that doesn't grow too big. *R. johnstoneanum's* sizeable scented white or pale yellow flowers make it very desirable. A tree-sized species I admire as much for its foliage as its flowers is *R. hodgsonii*. The dense trusses of cherry red flowers and smooth cinnamon bark are handsome and its noble leaves can be up to 30 centimetres long, dark green above, with a grey or sometimes fawn indumentum below. *R. leucaspis* is a dwarf shrub which needs a sheltered site and has lovely saucer-shaped white flowers, set off by chocolate-brown anthers, very early in the season. None of the Maddenii Series is completely hardy but *R. maddenii* subsp. *maddenii* Polyandrum Group – for convenience, *R. polyandrum* – is another plant well worth trying in a sheltered corner, for the sake of its sweetly scented flowers. *R. spinuliferum* is more interesting than beautiful, but its tubular red flowers are certainly striking. And of course the grove of the Muncaster hybrid is one of the great sights here each year. It is a wonderful plant.

2. Like many gardeners, I find that my attention often focuses on the new, the young, the rare or even simply the sick. For example, I'm very excited by some seedlings of *R. sinogrande*, which already have leaves 1 metre long. Then we have a young hybrid of *R.* 'Quaker Girl', × *R. macabeanum*, which has enormous flowers even at this early stage. I intend to spit on it and make it even bigger and better! And there's a poor dog-eared *Azalea mollis* in the kirkyard which I've mollycoddled back into a sort of life. It'll never amount to much but it has character and I'm fond of it.

3. I'm very pleased, too, with the *Nothofagus betuloides* seedlings from the single specimen beside the drive blown down in the storm of January 2005.

4. Another favourite is the Chilean evergreen *Eucryphia cordifolia*. There's a huge example of that on the drive – and it, too, has produced seedlings for us.

5. Another good Chilean evergreen is *Laurelia serrata*, the leaves of which are not only handsome but strongly aromatic. Don't sniff them if you suffer from asthma, though.

6. *Magnolia campbellii* subsp. *mollicomata* is simply glorious. It produces so many flowers that they seem to blot out the sky.

7. Something which reminds me of my beloved Highlands is the aspen (*Populus tremula*). In Gaelic its name means 'women's tongues'. I've planted five, for my wife and four daughters.

BRANTWOOD, CONISTON

With its land rising dramatically from Coniston Water to the high moorland behind, Brantwood enjoys what are often described as some of the finest views in England. It has also enjoyed a remarkable history. In the mid-nineteenth century it was owned by W.J. Linton, botanist (author of the first guide to Cumbrian ferns), radical political theorist and husband of the Victorian novelist Eliza Lynn Linton. In 1872 Linton sold the house to John Ruskin, a Victorian polymath, another radical (and idiosyncratic) political theorist and also an artist, art critic, social reformer and environmentalist.

Brantwood was Ruskin's home from 1872 to his death in 1900. During that time he greatly extended the house and estate while indulging his idiosyncratic ideas of garden making. In his later years, as he became increasingly frail physically and mentally, he eventually shared the house with his cousin Joan and her husband, the artist Arthur Severn, and their five children. She, too, created a

OPPOSITE The steps up to Ruskin's own favourite little garden – now known as the Professor's Garden – provide spectacular views down and out to the lake.

BELOW 'Come this way . . .' The inviting colourful profusion of a section of the Trellis Walk.

garden at Brantwood, but one very different in style from Ruskin's. In the words of Sally Beamish, who has been in charge of the gardens since 1988, 'Ruskin's was an experimental garden, a unique outdoor research and learning centre. Mrs Severn's was much more formal and "pretty", in the fashionable style of the day.'

For many years after the deaths of Ruskin and Arthur and Joan Severn, the 30 acres of garden were largely abandoned, but since 1988 Sally and her team (one full-time and two part-time assistants, plus local contractors and a team of volunteers) have been gradually reclaiming them from weeds. For the treatment of Joan Severn's areas – the High Walk area and the Harbour Walk – Sally uses the word 'restoration': 'Without full knowledge of the original plantings

we've tried at least to recreate her original vision.' For Ruskin's Northern Gardens, where she feels that the ideas he was exploring are the key element, she uses the word 'renovation': 'By this I mean that we've tried to bring his ideas alive for people today. Our real mission is to communicate Ruskin's inspiring ideas but we reward our visitors with the more straightforward pleasures of Mrs Severn's fine Victorian gardens.'

If visitors arrive by boat – as more and more do – they arrive at the Lower Gardens, where they are met by a combination of Mrs Severn's Victorian work and some 'New Ruskinian' thoughts on human beings' relationships with plants. A central orchard is flanked on one side by the Harbour Walk, an attractive spring avenue of

brightly coloured scented azaleas underplanted with narcissi (nowadays with the addition of unusual herbaceous plants, bulbs and grasses to extend the season), and on the other by the Trellis Walk. Until recently, this was edged by traditional herbaceous borders. Now, though, the borders are being reinterpreted 'Ruskinianly'. Each of nine trellised sections deals with an aspect of human interaction with plants. 'A particular plant may appear in more than one section,' Sally explains, 'to show how it's been used differently at different times.' Beyond is another even more Ruskinian garden, a herb garden called the Hortus Inclusus (the title of one of Ruskin's books). Devoted to British native plants, this is a 'learning garden', with the plants arranged by habitat, use and season.

OPPOSITE A striking section of the new Zig-Zaggy garden.

ABOVE A section of the recently replanted Terrace Walk.

Ruskin's Northern Gardens lie beyond and above the house. The most experimental section, the Moorland Garden, is still very much a 'work in progress'. Situated hundreds of feet above the house, it is criss-crossed by a maze of paths. Here Ruskin's ideas are being reinterpreted through various small-scale gardens. 'I want walking through this whole area to be like a walk through Ruskin's mind,' Sally says. So, for example, a 'geological garden' is being created at the bottom, while higher up, the garden's fern collection

(in honour of the house's one-time owner W.J. Linton) invites the close study of plant form to which Ruskin was devoted. At the top of the ascent Ruskin created a series of reservoirs, between which water was channelled. Characteristically, this was partly for practical purposes – 'He experimented up here with fruit trees and hardy strains of wheat: he was decades in advance of his time' – and partly for aesthetic ones, because he was fascinated by water and the patterns of its flow. The question of what to do with this area is still 'up for discussion'. 'It may just stay as a blank – a thinking space. And the making of a "thought garden" can be just as challenging as the creation of a traditional planted space.'

Ruskin's favourite area was closer to the house. He treated what became known as the Professor's Garden as a sort of idealized cottage garden, in which he experimented with plants he hoped would provide food not only for the local villagers' bodies but for their minds as well. It is still used for experiment – for example, trials of supposedly slug-resistant plants and experiments with cultivation using 'cast-off' materials, such as straw bales, fleece and bracken.

The most dramatic 'renovation' of Ruskin's ideas is a series of stone terraces rising straight from the car park and known as the Zig-Zaggy. 'Our interpretation of it was meant to shock,' says Sally gleefully. 'The starting point was a comment by Ruskin's friend W.G. Collingwood, who said that when he created these terraces Ruskin was thinking of the Purgatorial Mount in Dante's *Divine Comedy*.' So now the terraces are planted in a Ruskinian allegorical style, to represent the seven deadly sins. Pride, for example, is represented by what Sally calls 'the big "I am"s of the plant world', such as *Cordyline australis*, phormiums and *Euphorbia mellifera*, while Avarice consists of gold- or purple-flowered plants in a stumpery, the hollows of which will eventually be lined with copper. The idea is that you have to atone for each sin before ascending finally to paradise, in the form of one of the garden's few flat areas, excavated from the hillside and originally a tennis court.

After all this strenuous physical, mental and imaginative effort, visitors are rewarded with Mrs Severn's High Walk, a grassed terrace which makes a spectacular viewing point. The view is framed by her planting of conifers and *Rhododendron arboreum* hybrids and flanked by beds 'as formal as we can afford'. The flower colours are mostly greeny yellows and blues, 'the colours of the hills and sky', and the plants include violets and lilies 'because those were the names of Mrs Severn's two daughters'.

As we sit on a seat here and contemplate the mighty spread of landscape and garden, Sally says with a smile, 'I do hope Ruskin enjoys what we're doing with his land. He's not far away, in Coniston churchyard, so he's still keeping an eye on us.'

Brantwood is open daily from mid-March to mid-November, from 11.00 a.m. to 5.30 p.m, and Wednesday to Sunday from mid-November to mid-March, from 11.00 a.m. to 4.30 p.m. For more information, visit www.brantwood.org.uk.

PREVIOUS PAGES In late spring, bluebells carpet the ground beneath the trees in the ancient woodland behind Brantwood.

ABOVE Borrowed landscape with a vengeance: looking out over Mrs Severn's terraced High Walk and its huge old rhododendrons (early hybrids of *R. arboreum*) to the lake, Coniston village and the Coniston fells beyond. (The major ones, from left to right, are Dow Crag, Coniston Old Man and Wetherlam.)

High Cleabarrow, Windermere

High above Windermere in the heart of the Lake District Kath and Dick Brown have created a striking 2-acre garden without ever having had an overall plan. They have turned what they acquired in the early 1990s – an undulating expanse of lawn, a few small borders (including a flourishing rhubarb patch), a few sizeable trees, soil that was mostly poor, shallow and full of stone and shale, and one rocky outcrop, their own 24-metre-tall mini-mountain, which they call the Knoll – into a garden full of dramatic vistas and fine plants. This has been achieved by hundreds of Kath's individual 'decisions of the eye', in which she simply says to herself, 'Just here this plant looks right in itself and works well in the overall planting.'

The Browns operate as a classic gardening double act. Kath designs and plans the overall layout, and plants and maintains the beds; Dick constructs and maintains the hard landscaping (walls, paths, pond, pergola and so on), with occasional specialist help for large-scale or heavyweight tasks. Kath's main design tool, apart from her eyes, is the traditional length of hosepipe. The shapes of the curving island beds framing the central undulating, downward-sloping lawn, the terrace at the top of the slope and the man-made pond at the bottom of it all began life as a length of hosepipe draped along the ground. She then viewed it from the bedroom windows of the house, and adjusted it until a shape appeared which satisfied her eye. The Knoll, too, was turned into part of the garden in the same way. A network of informal terracing and winding paths was designed by both and then constructed by Dick. Now Kath's sympathetic planting of rhododendrons, azaleas and ferns leads to a summerhouse on the summit, which commands extensive views.

Despite being on poor soil, 700 feet up and exposed to bitter winds, the garden has become remarkably mature in a short time, through a combination of hard work and muck. The Browns are devoted compost makers and in spring and autumn feed their plants jumbo helpings of home-made compost with side orders of organic manure. 'If you want good results,' says Kath, 'you can't afford to skimp.'

Giant foliage – *Gunnera manicata* on the left, *Darmera peltatum* on the right – frames this view from the pond. The trees are a trio of white-trunked *Betula utilis* var. *jacquemontii* on the left and on the right with yellowing foliage Kath's favourite, *B.u.* var. *jacquemontii* 'Jermyns'.

The garden's design relies on a combination of planning and spontaneity. 'I don't plan the plantings in a bed in minute detail,' Kath explains, 'but I do decide in advance, long before I pick up a trowel or a spade, on the basic structural planting. First I make a list of plants I like that would be happy with the particular conditions of that bed. Then I think of plants from that list which will look happy in combination. If I've got that backbone – a sequence of plants which are all doing well and looking well together – I can afford to experiment with the rest.' In the same way, the planting throughout the garden is simultaneously naturalistic and sophisticated. Anything too formal would be out of place in such a rugged landscape but Kath still uses plants in carefully thought-out combinations. A combination will often include a tree; a shrub or two; several herbaceous clumps of different sizes, shapes and flowering times; and a cluster of bulbs at their feet. Nowadays, too, she tries to provide even greater coherence 'by giving each season its own particular palette of flower colours. In spring, I use lots of yellows and whites, while summer is pinks, mauves, purples, greys. Autumn tends to be oranges, deep reds and deep yellows.'

She manages to be a plant addict – 'I just love too many plants,' she admits cheerfully; 'I could plant for ever, particularly trees and shrubs' – while having a garden which is indeed a garden rather than a jungle of individual 'specials'. Although a devoted collector of dozens of different groups of plants, she is disciplined enough to use her rarities in ways which benefit the garden as a whole. Thus it is able to accommodate comfortably over a hundred different

Looking down the garden from the paved terrace by the house, with *Hydrangea macrophylla* 'Altona' in the right foreground and *Prunus* 'Collingwood Ingram' dominating the middle ground beyond.

varieties of unusual hardy geranium, for example, or an almost equally large collection of hostas, which thrive in Cumbria's cool moist conditions, as do hydrangeas, another group of plants she has energetically collected. There are also collections of euphorbias and hellebores, partly because she loves their architectural shapes but also because she believes they are good-value plants. 'We have a good framework of trees and shrubs but I also like to use a lot of plants which don't die away in winter. If your garden has extensive herbaceous planting, that can mean a lot of bare earth — and winters in Cumbria can be very long. Euphorbias and hellebores help to keep the garden looking clothed and happy. Most of them are hardy even this far north and this high up and they look good all the year round.'

Old-fashioned roses are another enthusiasm. There are Shrub roses in the mixed borders ('Real old roses do much better here than modern imitations of them,' Kath comments) and giant Climbers scrambling enthusiastically into the trees. The main collection, however, is to be found in a secret garden, reached through an archway in the main garden's beech hedge. This was previously a wilderness of brambles, docks and tree stumps which the Browns levelled and landscaped only a few years ago. Its box-edged beds are now filled with roses underplanted with campanulas, geraniums and

violas. Climbing roses mingle with honeysuckle and clematis ('my latest enthusiasm') over an arbour in one corner and over a gazebo in the centre. At first glance, such formality is surprising; nevertheless, it fits perfectly into the overall garden.

Kath confesses to spending at least two or three days a week in the garden (and she spends another day a week looking after a border in the walled garden at nearby Holehird – see page 94). Any visitor will agree that the results justify such commitment.

The garden is open by appointment to small groups – minimum eight, maximum fifty (telephone 01539 442808).

OPPOSITE An idyllic and apparently natural scene, but pond and planting have all been created by Dick and Kath Brown.

ABOVE The white trunks of *Betula utilis* var. *jacquemontii* act as a frame for a rich yellow seedling of *Kniphofia* 'Sunningdale Yellow' and, lightening the dark bower of foliage at the back, the frothy cream plumes of *Aruncus dioicus*.

FOLLOWING PAGE A dramatic combination of *Rosa* 'Bonica' and *Campanula lactiflora*.

Hosta 'Sun Power'

Acer palmatum 'Sango-kaku'

Cornus mas 'Aurea'

PLANT CHOICES

Kath Brown's choice of 'good-value' plants – plants which not only appreciate her moist acid soil but either have a particularly long season of interest or provide interest at difficult times of the year.

1. *Daphne bholua* 'Jacqueline Postill' grows to about 2 metres, has a wonderful scent and flowers for a long time from the end of January onwards.
2. *Jeffersonia diphylla* is a fine small herbaceous plant for moist woodland shade, with leaves which look like butterflies or bowties, white bowl-shaped flowers and, later on, good seed pods.
3. *Cornus mas* 'Aurea' makes a splendidly cheering show in spring, with its masses of yellow flowers on bare branches. Later the yellow foliage is also very effective.
4. *Cornus* 'Eddie's White Wonder' is perhaps even better, with an eye-catching display of big white bracts in spring and spectacular autumn colour.
5. *Rhododendron schlippenbachii* is a deciduous azalea with masses of lovely pink flowers in spring, either before or with the emerging leaves. In autumn it has the bonus that in a good year these pale green leaves 'turn' spectacularly, from yellow through orange to red.
6. *Betula utilis* var. *jacquemontii* 'Jermyns' I think is the best form of this indispensable birch. It has particularly fine white bark and striking butter-yellow autumn colour, and lights up the spring with its amazing catkins, which can be up to 12 centimetres long.
7. The large yellow leaves of *Hosta* 'Sun Power' are ideal for brightening a shady area.
8. *Rosa* 'Ispahan' is a lovely and sturdy old Damask rose which makes a substantial shrub and produces its highly scented flowers over a long period through late June and much of July.
9. *Acer palmatum* 'Sango-kaku' (also known as 'Senkaki') is indispensable for autumn and winter effects. Its leaves turn golden in autumn and in winter its young branches are a lovely coral red.
10. *Eucryphia lucida* × *cordifolia* is an outstanding member of this genus of handsome acid-loving large shrubs or small trees with a late summer and early autumn flowering period which makes them very desirable. It produces its substantial white flowers with conspicuous stamens in abundance even when quite young.

WINDY HALL, WINDERMERE

When David Kinsman and his wife, Diane Hewitt, arrived over twenty years ago at Windy Hall, high on the hills outside Windermere, their starting points were a ruggedly handsome old house and 4 rocky, sloping, thin-soiled, wind-lashed acres. Windy Hall's situation, their scientific training and very specific interests, plus the fact that their scientific jobs means they often have limited time to devote to it, have all determined the style of their garden.

Diane is an ecologist, David a geologist, and both have an interest in plant and animal conservation. The fields above and below are devoted to their own flock of rare breed sheep (David has written a book on Britain's ancient breeds of sheep) and they have designed the garden as a haven for birds and insects. It also houses two National Collections, of *Filipendula* and *Aruncus*. That is in part because the *Astilbe* National Collection is held at Holehird on the other side of Windermere, and since the three groups were

RIGHT The start of the quiet beauty of the mossy path through the Woodland Garden. This looks completely natural but is nothing of the sort.

BELOW The peaceful, wild Bird Garden pond and its islands.

LEFT Looking up at the house through the profuse planting of the sunken Best Garden.

FOLLOWING PAGE The ex-quarry in the Woodland Garden. With its carefully encouraged mosses and ferns and carefully positioned vertical and horizontal stones, it feels like a calm 'side chapel' to the 'central aisle' of the grand open space of the main glade.

once all classed as *Spiraea*, it makes sense to have the three collections close together.

Gardens made for worthily high-minded ecological or conservation reasons can easily be dull to look at. The garden at Windy Hall, however, is attractive in many varied if unconventional ways. The Kinsmans have combined an interest in the unusual with a keen eye for shape and structure and some clear thinking about the best gardening style for busy people with a large garden on an awkward site. In fact, the garden contains sections in several quite different styles, reflecting the site's wide range of possibilities and problems.

The section encountered first, running from the terrace in front of the house down to the road, is one of the most recently created, because it took years to find a solution to its difficulties. There were difficulties even after the Kinsmans had cleared away mountains of rubbish and weeds – something they have had to do throughout the garden. To start with, this is not a simple slope. It dips into a hollow, at the bottom of which is a drain. As a result, different parts of the area have very different characters. At the top is the best and most free-draining soil in the whole garden, while at the bottom there is a virtual bog. Other difficulties were the closeness of the house and two outstanding inherited plants, a huge *Acer palmatum* var. *dissectum* Dissectum Atropurpureum Group, at least fifty years old, and a shaggily gigantic old box (*Buxus*). The closeness of the house demanded a degree of formality and the two inherited plants demanded a design of which they would be the focus. So Diane and David have made paths, built walls, and installed semi-formal hedges and specimen eye-catcher plants to provide the structural skeleton of a design which distantly echoes the sort of garden style fashionable in the seventeenth century when their house was first built.

That the Kinsmans are scientists as well as plant enthusiasts has also had its effect here. The box tree was trimmed down into a modest shrub of a triclinic shape ('with three axes obliquely inclined towards each other', in dictionary-speak), because, says David the geologist, that shape is the lowest order of symmetry found in nature. Then, plant enthusiasm, an eye for beauty and some common sense meant that they have clothed the semi-formal framework of this section with dense but informal planting. The top of what they call the Best Garden, and the walls of the house itself, provide

homes for some surprisingly tender plants for such a high, inland, northern garden. They include *Solanum crispum*, *Carpenteria californica*, a cassinia, an ozothamnus and several tree heaths (*Erica arborea* and *E.a.* 'Albert's Gold'). Meanwhile, the lower, boggy portion is filled with moisture-lovers (many of them examples from the two National Collections).

It is not just here but throughout the garden that the planting is dense, because it acts as protection and support against the frequent high winds, and helps to save labour by suppressing weeds. And people with full lives, 4 acres of garden and more acres of sheep pasture have to take labour-saving seriously. That's why deadheading at Windy Hall is mostly done with a strimmer.

Above and behind the house, lawns have been made simply by clearing the ground and mowing whatever came up, until, finally, the major survivor became grass. However, obstinate patches of buttercups, clover and moss aren't just grudgingly accepted but embraced as appropriate and even beautiful. David says, 'We don't aim to make bowling greens. If people want to see a tidy garden, they'd better not come here.' Another labour-saving wheeze is to put grass clippings directly on to beds as mulch. This section also provides a good example of how to turn a difficulty into a delight: where there was only a thin skim of soil over rock, the Kinsmans often removed the soil to display the rock in its naked beauty.

Adjoining this area are, on one side, a vegetable and propagating garden and, on the other, the Bird Garden. This centres on a JCB-excavated pond, which David calls their 'insect factory', since it mass-produces food for birds. The pond contains two islands, with shapes and names that are typical of the Kinsmans' pomposity-deflating style. One, planted with *Gunnera manicata*, is eight-sided and hence called the Oct-o-gun. The other is boat-shaped and carries not one nameplate but a choice of two: this 'boat garden' is either Nancy or Marjory depending on whose mother is visiting.

If the Best Garden is Diane's particular territory, the 2-acre Woodland Garden is David's. By thinning and varying existing plantings of birch and conifers, he has created an area floriferous both in spring (with species rhododendrons and *Camellia* × *williamsii* hybrids) and, increasingly, in summer (with duplicate hydrangeas from the National Collection at Holehird), and graceful

and green throughout the year. He describes the felling, crown-lifting and planting involved as 'playing with the possibilities of space – and of available labour'. Space and possibilities were both considerably increased by the storm of January 2005. 'Yes, it caused a lot of damage – but in the long run the increased light will benefit the survivors.'

The most striking part of the Woodland Garden is its central grassy glade, with camellias on the shady side and autumn-colouring shrubs and trees, such as azaleas and *Acer japonicum* 'Aconitifolium', on the sunnier one. Beside that glade, an ancient small quarry has been turned into a Japanese-style area of moss,

ferns and stone. The massive uprights here, which look like altars or mini-Stonehenge-pillars, are actually traditional Lake District gate-stoops. A single, rounded, moss-covered stone at the quarry's entrance is, says the resident geologist, 'a glacial erratic'. In this quintessentially Lake District garden, it acts as a one-stone summary of Lake District history, and of how this fascinating garden has been achieved through an unusual combination of scientific interests and a keen eye for aesthetic effect.

The garden opens under the National Gardens Scheme and by appointment (telephone 01539 446238).

Polystichum commune

Kerria japonica

Viburnum × *bodnantense* 'Dawn'

PLANT CHOICES

David Kinsman and Diane Hewitt choose some of Windy Hall's most characteristic plants and explain their virtues.

1. Winter and early spring need not be a dull time for the garden. In various places we have plants for the surprise of their scent. For example, *Viburnum* × *bodnantense* 'Dawn', which has richly scented, whitish pink flowers, grey-green-leaved *Elaeagnus* × *ebbingei*, which has inconspicuous but sweetly scented flowers, the cowslip-scented *Corylopsis pauciflora*, plus *Lonicera fragrantissima*, and various sarcococcas, witch hazels (*Hamamelis* spp.) and tree heaths (*Erica arborea*, *E. canaliculata* and forms of them).

2. The most architectural plant we grow is *Gunnera manicata*. Three large clumps with their giant leaves over 2 metres high and almost as much across make a bold statement in the Bird Garden.

3. We have extended the season in the Woodland Garden by planting summer-flowering as well as spring-flowering trees and shrubs. Many have white flowers, such as halesia, styrax, stewartia, hoheria, clethra (wonderfully scented, particularly the sweet pepper bush *C. alnifolia*) and eucryphia. However, more than sixty species and cultivars of hydrangea provide a much greater range of late colour.

4. Windbreak shrubs are essential at Windy Hall. We have planted all the usual subjects but, having noticed that the January 2005 hurricane didn't damage any of our camellias, we have now planted a 20-metre windbreak hedge of *Camellia* 'Spring Festival'. This is an upright growing form, covered in spring with dainty pink flowers, which should be rather more interesting than most windbreak plants.

5. We tend to grow single-flowered rather than double-flowered forms of plants, as we find the former more elegant and pleasing. For example, the single-flowered wild species of *Kerria japonica* and the single-flowered *Ranunculus aconitifolius* are lovely, delicate plants compared with the more commonly seen double-flowered forms.

6. Mosses are an integral part of our garden. They grow so readily that it makes sense to use and welcome them rather than fight them. The moss paths in the woodland are dominated by the low-growing *Polystichum formosa*, while the rather taller *P. commune* is taking over much of the Quarry Garden. There are many other species in the garden and these have sparked an interest in getting to grips with moss identification.

HIGH CROSS LODGE, TROUTBECK

In 1990 Linda and Sydney Orchant were living near Manchester when they bought High Cross Lodge at Troutbeck in the heart of the Lake District. Originally they intended it to be a holiday cottage, but Linda was at once gripped by the beauty of the place and by its gardening possibilities. 'We just never went back to Manchester,' she says with a smile.

The house was built as the lodge to High Cross Castle and its estate. The serpentine culverted stream at the heart of the castle's Victorian gardens still runs through the Orchants' south-facing downward-sloping acre and Linda has made spectacularly successful use of it. In creating the garden she had no overall plan. Sydney says admiringly, 'It was just done in bits, but one day I looked up and bingo! It all fitted together!' She did, though, have clear preferences in plants and planting style. 'I'm interested in foliage plants and plants with a good architectural shape, rather than in flowers. Of course we have flowers, lots of them, but they're not what I think of as the garden's real point. And even more than most people I plant too closely, both because I hate bare earth and because at least then if something doesn't do well or needs to be cut down it doesn't leave a huge hole. Above all, though, I aim to grow what I like – and if the rules and the textbooks say I can't grow it, I break the rules and ignore the textbooks.'

Both her interest in architectural foliage and her cheerful flouting of the rule books are evident in her use of quite tender palms such as *Phoenix canariensis*, equally tender agaves and the bizarre South American pineapple plant (*Eucomis comosa*). Most of these are grown in pots, put out for summer and then sheltered under cover for winter. Many other plants that are unusual for a high inland northern garden, though, stay in the ground all year, including yuccas from the southern United States, New Zealand coloured phormium cultivars and drifts of the decorative Mediterranean onion relative *Nectaroscordum siculum*.

The serpentine remains of the original High Cross Castle water garden make a powerful contribution to the garden at High Cross Lodge.

OPPOSITE The stream, which was originally part of the castle's water garden, winding its way down the garden's slope.

LEFT Tender exotics in pots on the terrace, including a couple of palms (*Trachycarpus fortunei*) and an agave.

FOLLOWING PAGE Tree ferns seem to wave their fronds like giant waiters to point out the stepping stones to the summerhouse.

PAGE 93 Linda's 'pop-up' book mixed border, dominated – until the shrubs mature – by herbaceous planting. It rises up the slope in stages, each level higher than the one before.

Other examples of the risks Linda successfully takes are a dozen sizeable eye-catching specimens of the tree fern *Dicksonia antarctica*, spaced around the main lawn's central stone-walled circular bed. Most gardeners wouldn't dream of trying to grow this plant in the ground in inland Cumbria and the textbooks tell you to plant it in shade. Yet these specimens are growing and succeeding, year round, despite frosts, and in full sun. They survive even the hardest winters because Linda cuts off their fronds in late autumn and then protects their sides and crowns with straw inside a wire frame. And she realized that full sun in Cumbria is not the same as full sun in their native New Zealand. 'The fronds would probably scorch in New Zealand, perhaps even in Cornwall, but not with the sort of sun we get in Cumbria.' She also appreciated that shade in her tree-surrounded garden is mostly dry shade and what is crucial to tree ferns is regular moisture. Out in the open, the Cumbrian climate provides as much of that as any tree fern could want.

The circular bed in the lawn, irreverently known as the Bandstand, contains more examples of fine foliage plants and an equally fine disregard for the rules. Sun-and-drought-loving purple-flowered alliums and verbascums with huge felted grey leaves grow cheerfully alongside shade-and-moisture-lovers such as the delicate Japanese painted fern (*Athyrium pedatum* 'Japonicum'),

half a dozen different hostas, and ligularias with dinner-plate-sized leaves such as *L. przewalskii* and *L. stenocephala*.

Proving that Linda also loves flowers is an area on the left of the garden dominated by them. Above a fine slate-surfaced terrace, made from a rough grass slope and home to yet more architectural exotics in pots, is a triangular area divided into three by two cross paths and running steeply uphill. This has been designed to be 'like one of those pop-up children's books', with the profile of each section rising and falling and each section overtopping the one below it. The colours are mostly blues, purples and pinks, with occasional sculptural shrubs and trees to hold the composition together.

In the garden's top left-hand corner is a summerhouse, custom-made by local craftsmen. At this spot for reading, away from the phone, a place where the Orchants can enjoy a cooling evening drink or two, the several lines of stepping stones across the lawn converge. 'They just seemed to tie the whole shape of the garden together – but they also stop my slippers getting soaking wet when I come out first thing and walk around the garden while I'm still in my nightie,' Linda explains. Her remark is typical of the combination of style, fun and common sense which distinguishes her garden.

The garden opens under the National Gardens Scheme.

Brunnera macrophylla 'Jack Frost'

Fascicularia bicolor

Cercis canadensis 'Forest Pansy'

PLANT CHOICES

Linda Orchant's selection of favourite plants.

1. The shining silver leaves of *Brunnera macrophylla* 'Jack Frost' make wonderful ground cover, and the bright blue forget-me-not-like flowers are an added bonus. It is easy to grow in moist, rich, well-drained soil.

2. In moist shady places, *Pulmonaria* 'Blue Ensign' is ideal for following on from snowdrops.

3. *Hosta* 'June' (Tardiana Group) is my favourite of all my many hostas, because of the bright lemon and pale green midrib of its glaucous leaves, and because the slugs seem to leave it alone.

4. *Fascicularia bicolor* is a terrestrial bromeliad from Chile but grown in poor, sharply drained soil in full sun it is hardy even here in the central Lake District. The rosette of toothed blue-green leaves is attractive all year but during its summer flowering, when the inner leaves turn bright crimson around the cluster of stalkless blue flowers, it becomes stunning.

5. Growing to 1 metre or more, *Nectaroscordum siculum* looks like a cross between an allium and a lily and, though it is entirely hardy, fits perfectly into a tropical planting. The umbels of drooping cream flowers, flushed with pink and tinted green at the base, are charming. I'm told it can become a thug but it certainly hasn't been one here.

6. *Fritillaria persica* has exotic deep purple flowers, grey-green foliage and grows to about 1 metre. Despite coming from southern Turkey, in well-drained soil in full sun it is perfectly hardy here.

7. The South African honey bush (*Melianthus major*) has to spend its winters in a heated greenhouse at High Cross. It is worth that trouble, though, for the sake of its blue-green, boldly toothed foliage and scented terracotta-coloured flowers.

8. I grow the pineapple plant (*Eucomis comosa*) in pots because it is borderline hardy here. It is another plant which is worth a little bit of extra effort, for the sake of its stout stems topped by clusters of star-shaped flowers, each culminating in a tuft of leafy bracts.

9. *Acer palmatum* 'Sango-kaku' (syn. 'Senkaki') is a most striking Japanese maple. Its bright coral stems cheer up the worst of winter days. In spring the new foliage is orange yellow and in autumn it fades to soft yellow. In all seasons, it is lovely.

10. The beautiful deep purple, heart-shaped leaves of *Cercis canadensis* 'Forest Pansy' make it indispensable.

11. The variegated form of New Zealand flax (*Phormium tenax* 'Variegatum') has sword-like leaves with creamy yellow margins which make it a very striking specimen plant. And despite its exotic appearance it is very tough — certainly hardy down to at least −12°C. It is not for small gardens, as it makes a clump up to 3 metres by 3 metres.

12. The hardy palm *Trachycarpus fortunei* is a handsome architectural plant and I have found it completely bombproof in terms of resisting cold. It needs a sheltered site, though: otherwise wind tends to tatter the leaves.

HOLEHIRD, WINDERMERE

The Lakeland Horticultural Society's garden at Holehird outside Windermere appears to be the only large garden in Britain that opens to the public every day of the year yet is maintained entirely by voluntary labour. The members of the society are the staff: the planters, weeders, feeders, designers, propagators, scholarly keepers of its three National Collections, very professional makers of its plant labels, writers of its guide book, takers of the guide book's photographs, front-of-house staff who man (and woman) the reception desk and friendly wardens who answer visitors' questions. Since Holehird is slightly off the main tourist routes and does not come kitted out with the razzamatazz of a commercial undertaking, it is missed by many; yet its combination of beautiful setting, design and plants, together with the atmosphere generated by the busy volunteers, is very special,

Holehird's history is typical of the Lake District. Until the mid-nineteenth century it was simply a working farm in a spectacular situation, commanding fine views across Windermere to the Langdale Pikes. When such views suddenly became fashionable it was gentrified and aggrandized by three successive Manchester businessmen: John Lingard, John Dunlop and William Groves. In the 1850s Lingard commissioned a splendid mansion in the Gothic style from J.S. Crowther. In the 1870s Dunlop added to the mansion and created below it a series of terraces, while further up the hillside he constructed a 1-acre walled garden. When William Groves acquired the estate at the end of the century, the house was again extended, to a design by Dan Gibson. Simultaneously, the gardens were also extended. A stream was dammed to create a picturesque tarn below the terracing and Thomas Mawson added 160 feet of specialist glasshouses to the walled garden to provide homes for Groves' orchid collection. Later, he created a substantial rock garden on the hillside above. By the Second World War, however, like many such houses and estates, Holehird had become impossibly expensive to keep up. In 1945 Groves' son gave it to the county council, which leased it to the Leonard Cheshire Foundation, and for many years the garden was effectively abandoned. The rock garden and many of the paths were lost in undergrowth, brambles covered rare specimen shrubs and Mawson's glasshouses became so dilapidated that they had to be demolished.

OPPOSITE Part of the hydrangea collection, one of three National Collections held at Holehird.

BELOW The roses wreathing the gates are the magnificent white Rambler 'Rambling Rector' and the more restrained pink 'Debutante'.

Rescue came in 1969 with the foundation of the Lakeland Horticultural Society. In the years since, Holehird and the society have developed a symbiotic relationship, each relying on the other: the society is fortunate to have the garden as its home but equally the garden is fortunate to have the society as its 'curator'. And as the society has steadily grown over the years to its present membership of 1,700 it has taken in hand more and more of the garden. For the first ten years it was able to deal only with the Rock Garden and the slopes around it. In 1979 it assumed responsibility for the Walled Garden. Most recently, it has taken on the final piece in the jigsaw, the Lower Garden, including the terraces below the house.

The society now cares for 10 acres. That is a formidable undertaking for an organization made up mostly of amateur enthusiasts, however keen and gifted they are. There is, though, a useful smattering of members with professional training, including the society's current president and one of its founder members, Henry Noblett, who was for many years Head of Horticulture at Newton Rigg College near Penrith. The society tries hard to allow members who are active in the garden's maintenance to be what management jargon would describe as 'self-directed' – in other words, 'We don't push square pegs into round holes,' says Margaret Thomas, one of the society's stalwarts. 'People soon find out what they're really interested in.' The garden also tends to be a family affair: one person becomes interested and then before long that person's spouse is drawn in, with the result that there are many married couples among the society's active gardening membership.

Responsibility for the garden is divided between a series of 'teams' and a few determined individualists or specialized experts. For instance, there are quite large teams responsible for the finicky cultivation required in the alpine houses, for the design and maintenance of the major beds and borders and for constructional tasks involving serious 'lifting and shifting'. Individual specialists come in many different forms and apply themselves to many different areas, from propagation to compost making to irrigation. As a result of this system, and because there are so many different areas, each with its different requirements and possibilities, and so many different gardeners, each with his or her own different interests and

The view from Holehird in the low light of a February evening.

ideas, one of the fascinations of Holehird is that, although there is a garden committee to keep an eye on the overall effect, in many ways it has become a series of surprisingly personal creations. For example, the west border in the Walled Garden, supervised by Kath Brown, is very clearly 'hers' and has many of the hallmarks of her own garden at High Cleabarrow (see page 72). Other borders in other parts of the garden bear the equally individual marks of their particular creators and maintainers.

Holehird is a place to which both members of the LHS and visitors tend to become very attached – perhaps because of its element of quirky 'multiplied individualism', perhaps because it is so completely and heartwarmingly a voluntary affair, perhaps simply because Holehird consists of many high-quality gardens within a larger garden which is part of an outstanding landscape. Whatever the explanation for people's attachment to it, one result is that remarkable numbers of people leave donations to it in their wills. These have financed two striking recent memorial additions to the garden: a fine set of gates at one entrance to the Walled Garden and an armillary sphere in its centre. The feeling behind such donations – of profound gratitude for such a beautiful man-made garden so perfectly sited at the heart of such a beautiful natural one – is one any first-time visitor will rapidly understand and share.

The garden is open every day throughout the year. For more details about the garden and about membership of the Lakeland Horticultural Society, write to the society c/o Holehird Garden, Patterdale Road, Windermere LA23 1NP or telephone 01539 446008. There are occasional plant sales in the Walled Garden, described as 'low key' but in fact very well stocked. In early May the society holds an annual grand sale of thousands of plants – all propagated in the gardens, many of them rare, all of them desirable – at the nearby Lakes School, where there is more space.

Cornus controversa 'Variegata' makes an eye-catching centrepiece in the walled garden.

Desmodium tiliifolium

Rosa moyesii 'Geranium'

Geranium sanguineum var. *striatum*

PLANT CHOICES

Holehird's garden committee choose a dozen of their favourites from among the garden's hundreds of outstanding plants.

1. *Sambucus racemosa* 'Sutherland Gold' is a very attractive foliage shrub. The leaves are bronze when young and turn golden yellow as they age.
2. *Cornus controversa* 'Variegata' is often called the wedding cake tree because of its tiers of horizontal branches which are covered with creamy clusters of flowers in May and June. It makes a perfect lawn specimen and is small enough for quite small gardens.
3. *Aralia elata* 'Variegata' is grown at Holehird as a multistemmed small tree. Its huge doubly pinnate leaves are strikingly margined and blotched with creamy white. It has large panicles of white flowers in late summer and often colours well in autumn.
4. *Carpenteria californica*: in July the large white flowers, each with a central boss of golden anthers, are a spectacular sight, shining out against the glossy evergreen foliage. It needs a warm sheltered position this far north.
5. *Malus transitoria* was introduced from north-west China by William Purdom, whose father was head gardener at Brathay Hall in Ambleside. It is a delight in spring when it is swathed in white blossom, and it colours beautifully in autumn.
6. *Rosa moyesii* 'Geranium' is one of the best medium-sized Shrub roses, with brilliant geranium-red flowers in June and large, bright orange-red, pitcher-shaped hips from late summer into autumn.
7. *Liriodendron tulipifera* 'Fastigiatum' is an erect, columnar form of the well-known tulip tree. It is covered in yellow-green flowers in summer and the leaves turn butter yellow in autumn.
8. *Piptanthus nepalensis* is an evergreen Himalayan shrub which has large bright-yellow laburnum-like flowers in May and June. It benefits from some shelter in exposed gardens.
9. *Davidia involucrata* var. *vilmoriniana* has many popular names: handkerchief tree, ghost tree, dove tree. All are derived from the large white bracts which make it particularly eye-catching when they surround the tiny true flowers during May and June.
10. *Desmodium tiliifolium* is a Himalayan shrub belonging to the pea family which is covered with large panicles of delightful lilac-pink flowers throughout the summer.
11. *Geranium sanguineum* var. *striatum* is a delicately striped pale pink form of the bloody cranesbill. It has local connections, occurring naturally on the sand dunes of Walney Island off Barrow-in-Furness.
12. *Desfontainia spinosa* is a deceiver! For most of the year, this Andean evergreen shrub looks like a holly. Then in summer it gives away its exotic nature by suddenly producing showy red and yellow trumpet flowers. It needs a moist acid soil in partial shade and is not fully hardy, but it does well at Holehird.

BROCKHOLE, WINDERMERE

The story of Brockhole begins with a man named Henry Gaddum, a successful Victorian silk and textile magnate in Manchester. Like many self-made businessmen, he wanted to signal as loudly as possible the fact that he had arrived. One of the most fashionable ways for a Lancashire industrialist to do so then was to have architect Dan Gibson and Windermere-based garden designer Thomas Mawson make an appropriately grand house and garden in the Lake District for you. That's what Gaddum did — and the results are very much what visitors still see today. On a spectacular site rising from the shores of Windermere and offering views across it to the fells on the far side, Gibson designed for him a long low white house on top of a small hill. Below it, down to the lake, there extends one of the best and best-preserved gardens that Mawson ever created.

To take full advantage of the good drainage of the sheltered south-and-west-facing site he devised a series of terraces. These were cunningly planned so that you are led to look first down them, then out to the great expanse of water beyond, and finally across the lake to the dramatic skyline fells. It is a wonderful piece of 'garden theatre'. Even beyond the 10 acres of intensive garden, visitors with a serious interest in gardens or who simply enjoy a relaxing walk in a beautiful situation will find much to enjoy in Brockhole's additional 10 acres of wildflower meadow and 10 acres of woodland. Though the woodland consists mostly of native species planted for shelter, it also contains many fine ornamental specimens.

By the early decades of the twentieth century, Brockhole was one of the most impressive gardens in the county. After Henry Gaddum died, however, his family lost interest and sold it. After the Second World War it became for twenty years or more a convalescent home owned by the Merseyside Hospital Council, and suffered the usual fate of 'institutional' use. No serious new planting was done and maintenance of existing planting was fairly perfunctory. As a result, today the garden has many splendid trees and shrubs from the early twentieth century but a sad lack of trees and shrubs which should have been planted in the middle years of the century and be coming to maturity in the next two decades.

Rosa 'Bobbie James' wreathes the arch at the entrance to the Rose Garden.

In the early 1970s, Brockhole was acquired by the Lake District National Park Authority (LDNPA) and became its headquarters and main tourist information centre. Soon afterwards the garden began a process of resurrection. This started with a great deal of necessary catching-up, the most important part of which was the installation of many interesting new trees and shrubs. There also had to be a good deal of serious yet sympathetic alteration, because the garden's purpose now is completely different from its purpose when it was created. When Brockhole was a private house, the garden was for display to a few select friends of the family, and there were no more than a few hundred visitors a year. Nowadays it is visited each year by thousands —at the last count 170,000.

Inevitably, the alterations have involved a degree of compromise. The intention has been, on the one hand, to respect the fundamentals of Mawson's planting and design but, on the other hand, to accept that unavoidably changes were required, both to some of the details

of his design and to some of his plant choices. Originally, for example, the paths at Brockhole were made of pea gravel, an impractical surface for paths that have to deal each year with thousands of visiting children and hundreds of people in wheelchairs. So, after much discussion and heart-searching, the surface was changed to a more practical alternative: paving. Also when the LDNPA acquired Brockhole, the garden's peaks were almost entirely restricted to spring and autumn; in high summer it was not at its best and in winter it was asleep. Now visitors come above all in

high summer, but also right through the year, including winter. So the planting has had to be changed to extend the season of interest as far as possible.

The three main herbaceous borders provide perfect examples of changes of this sort. The planting is arranged so that their descent of the slope towards the lake follows the progression of the seasons through the year. The uppermost one is designed essentially for spring, and its colours are mostly pinks, blues and purples, provided by massed battalions of plants such as geraniums, penstemons, alliums and chelones. The middle border concentrates more on summer interest and, though it still has many pinks and purples, it adds many whites and yellows to the mix. The bottom border glows in autumn with the reds, bronze reds, purples, mauves and deep yellows of plants such as Kaffir lilies (*Schizostylis*), sedums, kniphofias, asters and nerines. Head gardener Susan Fryer is planning to reorganize these borders soon, though, in terms of a colour progression rather than a progression through the seasons, 'starting with hot colours on the top terrace and working down to whites, greens and lemon yellows on the bottom terrace'. Not that this is a garden which only provides colour. At times when flowers or even foliage colours are in short supply,

there are still the delights of the 'garden of the senses' which the LDPA has added at the end of the terrace by the house. Here, throughout the year, there are plants to smell and touch as well as to look at, and running water to beguile the ears.

The most exciting change, however, has been the extension of the range of the garden's plants. As appreciation has grown of how privileged Brockhole's climate is for an inland garden in the far north of England — south-facing, well drained and with the moderating effect of the adjacent lake — the planting has become more adventurous than it ever was before, even at its highest point under Henry Gaddum. As a result, visitors can experience the unexpected pleasure of seeing on this Cumbrian hillside flourishing examples of a wide range of semi-tender exotics, including Australian telopeas, callistemons and leptospermums and South American crinodendrons, desfontainias and embothriums.

Brockhole is open all the year round. It gets very busy as an information centre in the height of the summer season; spring and autumn are the seasons when the garden is likely to be least crowded. For details of opening times, telephone 01539 446601 or email hg@lake-district.gov.uk.

The wisteria on the retaining wall, trying to escape over the terrace above.

Stagshaw, Ambleside

Stagshaw is one of the Lake District's most lovely and peaceful gardens, with views that are spectacular even by Lake District standards. Yet although it lies only a few yards off the main A591 road through the area, it is little known or visited. Perhaps this is because it is high on the fellside just south of Ambleside, and signposted so discreetly and approached by such a tiny lane that it is easily missed.

Unlike most National Trust gardens, Stagshaw is both modern and the creation of a single person, Cuthbert ('Cubby') Acland, who until his retirement in 1973 was the National Trust's regional agent in Cumbria and lived in the cottages at the bottom of the garden. Both the cottages and the rough oak woodland on the hillside above them were part of the Wansfell estate, which was passed to the Trust in 1957, and it was out of that wooded hillside that Cubby Acland created his garden between 1959 and his death in 1979. He had spent his childhood on the Acland estate at Killerton in Devon (itself now a National Trust property), where earlier generations of his family had made an outstanding garden and collection of rare trees. As a result, woodland gardening was in his blood and, where most people would have seen at Stagshaw simply a pleasant piece of steeply sloping fell, he saw a potential garden. He devoted the last two decades of his life to the realization of that potential through a careful programme of felling, pruning and planting.

The site covers about 8 acres but can easily feel much more than that, since the hillside not only rises steeply but is sliced through by a series of ridges and valleys, including one which contains a beck dashing downhill through alternately gently gurgling and wildly roaring miniature waterfalls. And this is not a garden where what nature provided has been landscaped to fit a predetermined plan. Footpaths follow the existing – and often precipitous – contours. Where occasionally there are more or less horizontal patches of ground, the opportunity has been seized to create miniature grassy glades, which often contain a seat from which to survey an exceptional view or a particular combination of plants. In short, this is a garden in which the art lies in concealing its own skill.

A characteristically natural-looking but completely man-made corner of Stagshaw, with a path winding invitingly onwards through banks of camellias (pink 'Donation' on the right) and rhododendrons.

It aims, despite its profusion of exotic trees and shrubs, to look entirely natural and 'untouched by human hand'.

In spring and early summer Stagshaw's star turns are Cubby Acland's plantings of rhododendrons of every conceivable kind and combination. He planted species, he planted hybrids. He planted those with huge leaves and those with tiny leaves. He planted those which will become trees (in some cases, such as the noble *R. thomsonii*, they already have) and those which will always remain dwarf. And he planted them both as individual specimens and as substantial groups. Always, though, they were sensitively arranged in terms of flower colour and flowering times. Combinations of colours are often dramatic here, but they never shout at each other.

The 'supporting cast' at this time of year consists largely of camellias and magnolias, many of them now of impressive size and flowering profusely. There is also an unexpected and highly effective small grove of tree-sized specimens of *Griselinia littoralis*, the dark contorted limbs of which make a powerful impact in every season of the year, though rather an eerie one, particularly when seen through a swirling autumn mist. The garden contains not just tree-sized exotic shrubs but exotic trees. Sensibly, the exoticism is not too extreme, given Stagshaw's high and exposed situation. So the trees chosen to supplement the original oaks are predominantly species of maple, birch and cherry, with the occasional unusual conifer and a few single specimens of other desirable species.

In summer, Stagshaw is still beautiful and peaceful, but it is in its most 'fallow' period, when the majority of flowers have gone yet foliage colour is still to begin. (Perhaps another reason why Stagshaw is so little known is that visitor numbers are not at their peak at its two best periods.)

Spectacular though spring and early summer are here, if anything this is a garden which is even better in late October. Then, the extravagant rich reds and browns of dying leaves – supported by some choice late-flowering trees: in particular, a number of fine eucryphias – contrast with the vivid greens of still-lush grass and the still-fresh fronds of the garden's many ferns. The beck roars and bubbles down the hillside, the lake glitters from just beyond the garden's trees and the fells shimmer in the distance. At that time of year it is difficult to imagine a more beautiful garden.

OPPOSITE This dramatic display of multicoloured azaleas and dwarf rhododendrons around the amphitheatre-like main clearing is one of Stagshaw's great sights in spring.

ABOVE After an early November rainstorm the arching elegance of evergreen ferns (probably *Dryopteris affinis*) shows up beautifully against the racing torrent of the beck.

In any season, though, Stagshaw is not only beautiful but also offers the rare pleasure for a National Trust garden in the centre of a major tourist hotspot of being so little visited that it has the feeling of being not only a very personal creation but, for the duration of your visit, your own private possession.

The garden is open daily during May and June and by appointment between July and October (telephone the National Trust's north-western headquarters on 01539 435599). The garden's car park has room for only three or four cars at most. Much the best idea is to park in the car park at the head of the lake and then enjoy the short lakeside stroll southwards until you reach the sign pointing up to Stagshaw's approach lane.

MATTHEW HOW, TROUTBECK

When Rosemary Griffiths spotted that a child visiting Matthew How was deeply bored by her mother's enthusiasm for plants, she took her off on a tadpole-gathering trip to the pond, during which both adult and child became wet, muddy and dishevelled. Chatting afterwards, the girl revealed that when she grew up she wanted to become a ballet dancer. 'And what', she asked with total seriousness, 'do you want to be when you grow up?' I know just what that girl meant. Although John and Rosemary Griffiths are past retirement age, they have a youthful zest for life, a puckish sense of fun and an individual sense of style, all of which are reflected in the delectable garden they have made around Matthew How, their cottage at Troutbeck in the heart of the Lake District.

In the late 1970s when they arrived, it was a wasteland. The cottage had once been the village pub, the Jolly Dragoon, and they had to remove sixteen skiploads of old bottles from the patch beside the house. The rest of the garden was a run-down smallholding. Its geography and soil added to the problems. The small area in front of the cottage is flattish but the main garden behind it zooms rapidly and erratically upwards. From the rough grass here they created, by repeated mowing and feeding, six small lawns. Mowing these is John's job and, since powered mowers cannot cope with their undulations, he relies on two antique hand-mowers. As for soil, there hardly is any. At a spade's depth you are into rock. When the Griffithses attempted to bury their dog, Tess, they were unable to excavate to the necessary depth and had to call in a strong-armed neighbour with crowbar and pickaxe to finish the job.

The site presents two great advantages, though. It faces south-east so, given some shelter planting against wind, it is relatively warm and, because of the slope, well drained. And it offers spirit-lifting views across the valley to the skyline fells of the High Street range. Even so, what holds the garden together is not those 'givens' but Rosemary's very individual style.

The miniature front garden is a model of formal restraint, leavened with unexpected twists. It was designed as 'a resting point', somewhere to allow you quietly to absorb the view rather than somewhere that would attempt to compete with it – hence the

This slightly outraged-looking topiary bird (note the eyes) seems to be guarding the view over the front garden and the ancient billowing box hedge to the High Street fells beyond.

formal box hedges and box 'shapes' in gravel beds, each shape with a circle of differently coloured and sized gravel around it. 'I think of them', she laughs, 'as being like wedding cakes on stands being "presented" to you.' This formality is offset by the roller-coaster undulations of an ancient box boundary hedge, the line of which she tries to make echo the skyline fells. The cloud shapes on its outer surface, on the other hand, come partly from design and partly from skilfully used serendipity – for instance, when a lorry crashed into it the resulting dents became yet more bosomy curves. 'The hedge has a mind of its own,' Rosemary says. 'It has evolved its own shape. As I garden unseen behind it, I love hearing people's comments. I've heard it described as a herd of elephants,

a train, a dinosaur and even as something written in hieroglyphs.'

Behind the house, on the steep uneven hillside, Rosemary has used the natural undulations to create a garden of episodes. Meandering paths and flights of informal steps lead to a series of sheltered nooks, often with a seat tucked into a corner from which to contemplate the views down the garden and out across the valley. This is essentially a garden of trees and shrubs, with rhododendrons, camellias, magnolias and acers predominating. Most have clematis snaking through them to add interest after their hosts' flowering season is over. Often two or three occupy a single shrub, as when *C. heracleifolia* and the bell-flowered *C.* 'Alionushka' embrace a buddleja. Then, around and at the feet of the trees and shrubs, carefully chosen herbaceous and bulbous

planting is tucked in. For example, pale yellow narcissi flower beneath a sheltering arch of the pale green filigree foliage of a miniature *Acer palmatum* var. *dissectum*. On a larger scale the formal blue ball of a clipped *Eucalyptus gunnii* is emphasized by the pink rhododendron and the deep red acer poised behind and above it. Such discriminating combinations are typical of Rosemary's sensitive skill.

Topiary such as that 'balled' eucalyptus has become one of the garden's specialities. A recent example is a small yew clipped into a miniature version of Anthony Gormley's *Angel of the North*. To Rosemary's delight, one child visitor said, 'This is much better, so this should be the *Archangel of the North*.' And that is now the proud name on the hand-painted stone at its foot. Even the darkest shade is

Looking down the orchard to the village below, through the orchard's espaliered apple trees and some of Rosemary's 'trademark' blue bars and decorative blue tops.

ABOVE A sudden open green space provides a welcome and well-judged change of mood in this densely planted garden. 'Sometimes,' says Rosemary, 'you just want a space.' That is also why the large jar is deliberately left unplanted.

RIGHT Looking down and back towards the cottage through one of Matthew How's characteristic combinations of spectacular flowers (red rhododendron, pink camellia and white magnolia) and strong shapes from clipped evergreens.

FOLLOWING PAGE Each spring the entrance to the garden is decorated with a welcoming display of pots and wooden tubs. The tubs' iron supporting bands are painted in Rosemary's trademark 'Venetian blue' and each tub is filled with an explosion of her beloved tulips.

enlivened by what Rosemary describes as her 'torches of the night': self-seeded yews which she has clipped into sombre torch-like shapes. Not only yews but even the tiniest plants are 'topiarized' into light-hearted sculptures. One small ornamental grass has had its 'hair' turned into a couple of plaits, while a stone in front of it has become the creature's face, with shells for its eyes and mouth.

Such visual fizz is not provided just by plants. Vertical poles erupt unexpectedly from the beds throughout the garden. Some are decorated with blue horizontal or vertical lines. Some are topped by a seashell, others by a wooden duck. Rosemary laughingly refuses to explain why. 'I must be in my Blue Period,' she jokes. Then more seriously she asks, 'Why do we always need an explanation? Sometimes no explanation is the explanation.'

The charms of Matthew How also include its stylish Pekin bantams and its current lurcher, Mattie, plus a vast wildlife population, among which are nuthatches, pied flycatchers, goldcrests, woodpeckers, owls, bats and red squirrels. Life here is still very much a form of country life, albeit far removed from that lived by those long-ago regulars of the Jolly Dragoon.

The garden is open by appointment during May and early June (telephone 01539 433276).

Forget-me-not

Trillium grandiflorum

Schizostylis coccinea

PLANT CHOICES

Rosemary Griffiths' choices of some essential plants to help create a stylish yet relaxed country garden.

1. The acers are indispensable – a genus for all seasons. Different members provide spectacular colour, interesting bark, lovely leaf form or a handsome overall shape. Some even provide all those things. Particular favourites here are *A. griseum*, *A. japonicum* 'Aureum' (aka *A. shirasawanum* 'Aureum') and *A. japonicum* 'Vitifolium'.
2. Box and yew hedges and topiary give structure to a garden – and they can give it humour, too. In frost or snow or in dusky misty light they also create a very special atmosphere.
3. All the bamboos are wonderful for adding lightness and movement and a touch of the exotic.
4. Plants don't need to be rare to be desirable. What is lovelier than drifts of snowdrops, their innocent charm a harbinger of spring, or a bank of dainty evocative violets, or carpets of bluebells in old woodland?
5. Aquilegias and forget-me-nots, too, are so much part of English country and cottage gardens. They are plants to be sown randomly and in abundance.
6. Hellebores are indispensable for bringing charm and colour to what might otherwise be a drab time of the year.
7. A little later, I love *Trillium grandiflorum*, for its unique form, purity and shy scent.
8. *Abutilon × suntense* is a charming May-time star. It is hardy here in sheltered corners.
9. The lily-flowered tulips have a wonderful grace and lissom beauty.
10. *Anemone hupehensis* 'Hadspen Abundance' is a stately and long-lasting friend in the garden in autumn.
11. The schizostylis are very easy to grow and all give welcome brilliant colour in October and November. They look particularly good against a backcloth of red-berried plants.

Copt Howe,
Great Langdale

Professor Bob Haszeldine and his late wife Peggy bought Copt Howe over two decades ago. The solid stone house is set on 2 acres of what was then rough fellside, high on Silver Howe in the dramatic Langdale Valley. Sloping at forty degrees, these acres consisted of huge immovable boulders, scree and a thin, rain-eroded apology for soil. There was no shelter from storms, and temperatures here not infrequently fall as low as −10°C. However, the mountain views were irresistible and the Haszeldines relished the challenge of creating a garden here.

They transported soil, full-grown trees and shrubs, and numerous stone troughs from their previous garden in Cheshire. Then they began to make beds, edged with stone walls built from the scree, to allow them to add acidic topsoil without it being washed away. The other vital early step was to create shelter planting – mostly rhododendrons and quick-growing conifers – to protect the garden's most exposed aspects. Overflowing becks were rerouted or culverted, while a network of winding paths, metre-high stone-built retaining walls and sections of terracing threaded its way across the relentlessly steep and irregular terrain, carefully positioned so that the wind seldom has a direct path through.

Over the years, they acquired more and more soil, supported by vast quantities of home-made compost. Soil introduced here is hand-mixed to a very particular specification. Compost, peat, leafmould and lots of grit provide a free-draining but moisture-retentive and humus-rich medium. Nitrogen, phosphorus and potassium levels are deliberately kept low so that plants send down deep roots in search of food and don't make lots of soft new growth, which would easily be damaged in Langdale's harsh climate.

Modifications of the site have always respected its essential shape and spirit. In this informal mountain garden, areas of quite dense woodland alternate with sudden open glade-like spaces. The untutored eye might easily suppose that this 'just happened' but it is in fact the conscious – and continuing – creation of a discriminating plant

OPPOSITE Looking down from the fellside over Copt Howe and its garden to Bowfell and the Langdale Pikes at the head of the valley.

BELOW A springtime path towards the edge of the garden, with the Langdale fells beyond.

FOLLOWING PAGES *Eleutherococcus sieboldianus*, a red acer cross, and *Ulmus glabra* 'Jacqueline Hillier' make a perfect frame for this view of the Langdale Pikes.

LEFT The trunk of this *Acer palmatum* var. *dissectum* was deliberately and repeatedly split when it was young to make it multistemmed, while its young leaves are encouraged to grow directly from the gnarled and mossy stems. The end result is an eye-catching combination of colour and structure.

lover with a keen eye for both good plants and good combinations. Even at over eighty Bob is still adding to the garden; for instance, he has recently expanded the area devoted to alpines. 'I've been in research all my life,' he says: 'I'm used to having many projects on the go at once and remain as curious as ever about what lies round the next corner.' Development on terrain as rugged as this involves a lot of hard physical graft and he acknowledges gratefully the contribution of Langdale native Joe Wrathall, who has helped in the garden for many years.

Bob's method for designing new plantings is as idiosyncratic as the rest of his approach. He propagates and grows on a wide range of trees, shrubs and perennials, often to quite large sizes. When a new area becomes available or when an old one is to be replanted, he selects possible candidates from that stock. Positioned on site, sunk in the ground but still in their pots, they are left there for as much as a year until he is satisfied that they are in suitable positions. If he is not happy with his first attempt, he reshuffles everything. He thinks of what he does as 'painting with plants': creating satisfying shapes and combinations of colour and leaf form in relation to a specific and unique piece of ground, while bearing in mind the special needs of each plant.

However, once the plants are in their permanent positions, in a suitable site and with suitable soil, they are left to thrive or fail unaided. 'I'm a scientist – I don't believe in fighting against nature very much.' The planting is unusually close, so that individuals shelter each other against wind and cold and weeds are minimized. Weeds (and maintenance) are also minimized by the generous use of mulches. As a result, hundreds of different plants, from giant trees to tiny bulbs, flourish on this once bleak site. Many have been grown from seed, cuttings or grafts, or acquired by permitted collection in the wild, having impressed Bob on his travels abroad while in pursuit of his main hobby, mountaineering and trekking.

Among Copt Howe's stars in early spring are hellebores, flourishing in every shade of green, white, cream, yellow, pink and purple. Some are solid single colours; others are blushed or delicately patterned in secondary tones. Some are hybrids of Bob's own raising; others are the plants' self-hybridized creations. Either way, in his cheery phrase, 'they're all bastards'. Later, the range of meconopsis is equally striking, with twenty or more species or forms, mostly grown from expedition seed. Collections of galanthus, cyclamens, trilliums, dactylorhizas, cardiocrinums, nomocharis, hepaticas, alliums and lilies give colour, contrasts of foliage and scent throughout the season, while alpine beds house many miniature treasures.

The garden's backbone, though, is its outstanding collection of trees and shrubs. Innumerable conifers, from natural dwarfs to forest giants, include many with such fine shapes and foliage colour that Bob considers them 'natural works of art' – for example, blue-grey *Cedrus atlantica* 'Glauca', light grey *Picea pungens* 'Hoopsii', vivid yellow *P. orientalis* 'Skylands', glowing green *P. breweriana* and the rugged bristlecone pine (*Pinus aristata*). Other trees and shrubs here include *Arbutus andrachnoides*, a russet-barked *Rhododendron* 'Loderi' and the wedding-cake-shaped *Cornus alternifolia*. If the conifers are Copt Howe's solid citizens, then its spectacular show-offs are its 150 or more acers.

Bob's passion for acers means that there are ones here for every possible purpose and season: for year-round bark, spring foliage and of course autumn colour. His favourites include russet-barked *A. griseum* with orange-scarlet autumn foliage; the hardy and compact *A. shirasawanum* 'Aureum', 'which makes a fine specimen plant'; *A. aconitifolium*, whose fern-like foliage turns carmine in autumn; and *A. palmatum* 'Beni-hime', which has leaves that change from spring pink to green to autumn pink and finally rich red. The dwarf forms of *A. palmatum* are just as spectacular – for example, 'Red Pygmy', whose long, fringed red leaves make it, Bob says appreciatively, 'an aristocrat', the 'unforgettable' bonsai-like 'Shishigashira', and 'Higasayama', with scalloped leaves edged in pink.

The acers' spring and autumn fireworks, the conifers' evergreen elegance, the spring-time extravaganzas of hellebores and meconopsis: these are just three of the many exceptional experiences offered by this exceptional garden in an exceptional setting.

Copt Howe is a garden full of both little treasures, cosseted either in troughs or in specialist corners, and of the mighty aristocrats of woodland gardens, such as this fine magnolia.

Copt Howe opens regularly under the National Gardens Scheme. For recorded weekly information about other open days, and to arrange group visits, which are welcome by appointment, telephone 01539 437685.

Picea pungens 'Hoopsii'

Cercis canadensis 'Forest Pansy'

Acer shirasawanum 'Aureum'

PLANT CHOICES

Bob Haszeldine prefers just to list names rather than give descriptions. 'That way I can perhaps sneak in a few more plants — and if people are really interested they can easily look up the descriptions.'

Trees and shrubs:
1. *Acer shirasawanum* 'Aureum'
2. *Prunus serrula* (syn. *P. tibetica*)
3. *Embothrium coccineum* 'Norquinco'
4. *Metasequoia glyptostroboides* 'Gold Rush'
5. *Cercis canadensis* 'Forest Pansy'
6. *Betula ermanii* 'Grayswood Hill'
7. *Aesculus indica × neglecta* 'Erythroblastos'
8. *Picea pungens* 'Hoopsii'
9. *Arbutus andrachnoides*

Perennials:
1. *Meconopsis* 'Lingholm'
2. *Helleborus orientalis*
3. *Nomocharis* species such as *N. pardanthina*, *N. meleagrina* and *N. saluenensis*
4. *Cardiocrinum giganteum*
5. *Trillium grandiflorum*
6. *Hepatica × media* 'Ballardii'
7. *Tropaeolum speciosum*
8. *Dactylorhiza* species such as *D. elata* and *D. maculata*
9. *Anemone trullifolia*

Rydal Mount and Rydal Hall

The very different gardens at Rydal Mount and Rydal Hall in the heart of the Lake District are separated by only 100 yards of fell and a narrow lane. The substantial Rydal Hall estate has been owned for centuries by the Fleming or le Fleming family, and in the early nineteenth century Lady Diana le Fleming added to it by acquiring Rydal Mount and its 4 acres of land. In 1813 she rented this to the poet William Wordsworth, who lived there until his death in 1850. It is he of course who is responsible for today's thousands of visitors to Rydal Mount – and it was also he who was largely responsible for the design of the garden which frames the house.

That design was very much in the style of the much larger gardens then around neighbouring Rydal Hall. As early as the mid-seventeenth century the dramatic fellside landscape above and below the hall had been one of the first in Britain to have its picturesque attractions recognized and enhanced. Its then owner, Sir Daniel Fleming, planted trees to emphasize the views down the valley to distant Windermere; and he built a terrace in front of the house, from which they could be seen to their best advantage. Above the house, he or later eighteenth-century Flemings carved out a winding path, with stone steps and 'viewing stations' which snaked along beside a beck and its many miniature waterfalls. Later, a circular walk was created, which looped inland at the highest point and then descended to the house through rhododendron-rich Birk Hagg woods. It was certainly Sir Daniel who built what he called the 'grot', a summerhouse from which to view a particularly romantic combination of beck, natural waterfall and picturesque bridge. He wrote proudly of his 'pleasant Gardens, Orchards, Walks, a Pond, a Mill and a Grot. . . with a pleasant Prospect over most of ye Vale and over part of Winandermere ye greatest standing water in all England'.

The garden Wordsworth created at Rydal Mount 150 years later was still in that Picturesque style, the aim of which was to respect the natural beauty of the landscape while at the same time enhancing it. Of garden design he said, 'The invisible hand of art should

A fine shrub border along the path around the upper edge of the lawn at Rydal Mount. The rhododendrons are much later than Wordsworth's time – probably early twentieth century.

ABOVE The path along the upper terrace to Wordsworth's summerhouse, tucked into the fellside high above the lake.

OPPOSITE The view out to Rydal Water, which Wordsworth loved. In his day more of the lake would have been visible because the trees would have been much smaller.

everywhere work in the spirit of Nature and of Antiquity, her sister and co-partner.' He exercised his own artful hand on Rydal Mount's naturally sloping 4 acres for thirty-five years. These acres lie partly in front and partly to the west of the house. The area in front formed a natural 'promontory', with fine views down to Windermere (it was used for many centuries as a site for warning beacons). To the side of the house he created a long main lawn, above which, over the years, he constructed a series of linked terraces. Midway along the

uppermost one he built a stone summerhouse for contemplation, with its back cosily tucked into the hillside. From the terrace beyond it there are glimpses of Rydal Water below. He described how he used to stride back and forth here while mentally composing his later poems:

> A Poet's hand first shaped it; and the steps
> Of that same Bard – repeated to and fro
> At morn, at noon, and under moonlight skies
> Through the vicissitudes of many a year –
> Forbade the weeds to creep o'er its grey line.

In terms of its basic structure, the garden remains much as Wordsworth left it a century and a half ago. The detailed planting is now largely from after his time but it remains true to his spirit and to

his feeling that in an area of such natural beauty a garden should harmonize with, not stand out against, its surroundings. His own prescription was simply 'lawn, and trees carefully planted so as not to obscure the view'. Add 'shrubs' to trees and that is very much the sort of garden visitors see today. It is a quiet, unostentatious place, but one which is richly atmospheric.

In the early twentieth century, however, a dramatic change of style occurred at the larger garden down the hill. Rydal Hall had by then become a substantial mansion and the Edwardian le Flemings decided that it needed a much grander and more formal setting. The man they turned to for its design was the local favourite of the time, Windermere-based Thomas Mawson. He produced a piece of formal mock-classical dignity typical of the period, with terraces subdivided by flagstoned paths, surrounded by balustrading and punctuated by seats, pillars, geometric box-edged beds, sculpted yews, impressive urns, a grand fountain and a grander grotto. It was also typical of the period that what appeared at first glance to be a vastly expensive construction in stone was in fact much more cheaply constructed out of pre-cast concrete. Typical of Mawson himself was the combination of grandeur with touches of homeliness.

The terrace seats, for example, were sheltered by a series of miniature pergolas, which had imposing pillars as their uprights (also made out of concrete) but simple rustic-looking logs as their horizontal top-pieces. The planting of this grand scheme consisted of vividly coloured exotic bedding plants for high-summer display, while the urns along the terrace walls were planted with bold vertical eye-catchers such as cordylines.

As with many such gardens, its heyday was sadly brief. From the 1940s onwards the hall was let to tenants who, understandably, failed to cope with its considerable maintenance requirements. By 1970 when the Diocese of Carlisle bought the hall with its garden and 30 acres or so of surrounding woodland, much serious damage had occurred. The culprits included neglect, insensitive attempts at renovation, subsidence, frost and vandalism. Parts of the upper

ABOVE Looking across the restored Mawson garden from the steps leading up to it.

RIGHT Restored Edwardian splendour now frames the view down the valley towards Windermere.

terrace had sunk, pillars and balustrading had cracked or been forced out of alignment and the lower 'grotto' below the main terrace had suffered so much damage from leaking water that stalactites had formed on its ceiling. The final insult was that thieves had spirited away many of the Mawson urns.

In the late 1990s, the Church at last took determined steps to rescue the garden. The necessary (and very substantial) funds were raised. Mawson's original design sheets were found, and many of his moulds for steps and balustrading were discovered, hidden in the hall's cellars. Head gardener Tom Attwood was appointed and, though no Mawson planting plans had survived, landscape architect Simon Bonvoison prepared schemes for the terrace beds based on plantings from other Mawson gardens. Even the walled garden high on the fell above the house is being restored for use as a community vegetable garden, while the out-of-control trees and shrubs along the picturesque beckside walk have been thinned and reduced. The restoration work began at the end of 2005 and progressed with such speed that by the end of 2006 all the hard landscaping elements of the formal garden had been repaired. The new planting there is already starting to make its intended impact.

So visitors to Rydal's two fine gardens nowadays encounter two quite different gardening styles, co-existing oddly but effectively almost side by side in this corner of Lakeland, which has been richly endowed both by nature and by human endeavour.

The garden at Rydal Mount is open daily from March to October from 9.30 a.m. to 5.00 p.m, and in November and February from 10.00 a.m. to 4.00 p.m., except on Tuesdays, when it is closed. It is closed during December and January. For more information, telephone 01539 433002 or visit www.rydalmount.co.uk.

The garden at Rydal Hall is open to individuals from 10.00 a.m. to 4.00 p.m. every day, 'provided visitors respect the peace and quiet of this place of retreat'. You can park by the Bulley Barn (follow the signs). The Ramblers' Teashop in the hall grounds is open every day of the year from 10.30 a.m. to 4 p.m. For more information, write to Rydal Hall, Ambleside, Cumbria LA22 9LZ, telephone 01539 432050 or email mail@rydalhall.org.

PARCEY HOUSE, HARTSOP

In its spectacular setting opposite Brotherswater at the head of Patterdale, Dick and Liz Clark's densely planted and elaborately terraced acre at Parcey House at first glance looks almost effortlessly beautiful. However, while Liz happily admits that 'the possibilities of the garden' were for her a major inducement to moving here twenty years ago, those possibilities were made reality only by enormous amounts of hard work. She still reckons to spend three full days a week in the garden. As Dick says, 'No site could be more demanding or body destroying. It's a garden which is always calling to you.'

What made the creation of this garden such hard work was the combination of site, soil and climate. The Clarks acquired what had originally been a small farmhouse, plus the land immediately above and below it. Previous non-farming owners had left a legacy of some good trees and shrubs (camellia, cherry, amelanchier, liriodendron, a fine metasequoia) but had left quite unmodified the steep grassy slope above the house in which some of them had been planted. Liz explains, 'In the beginning I just walked around with a lawnmower trying to cut the easiest paths. It was daunting even doing that.' To her 'skeleton' of paths she painstakingly added 'flesh' in the form of a series of stone-built terraced beds, working upwards from the house towards the top of the slope (which, twenty years on, she still has not quite reached). She has had no hired help, except recently for one bit of wall and one stretch of path.

Her terraces serve two purposes. They help prevent soil being washed away to the bottom of the garden by Hartsop's 2 metres of rain a year; and they allow her to add more depth of decent soil to the site's natural few stony centimetres. (That's why composting is a major industry here, which neighbouring farmers help with generous loads of muck.) Rain is not the only climatic problem they face. They are at the meeting of two valleys and from time to time winds come down both simultaneously, creating a devastating whirlpool effect. 'Trees grow surprisingly straight but we do get breakages.' On the other hand, the site offers some practical as well as picturesque advantages. 'At least rain runs away quickly'; and, they point out, 'We're surprisingly sheltered by projecting hillsides. It's actually much more exposed lower down the village.'

OPPOSITE A quiet seat by the pond. In the foreground are the large leaves of white-spathed *Lysichiton camtschatcensis*, *Primula* Bartley hybrids, *Trollius × cultorum*, blue and white-flowered varieties of *Iris laevigata*, and *Carex riparia* 'Variegata'.

ABOVE *Rhododendron* 'Pink Pearl' alongside the paths leading to the lower, more level, parts of the garden.

They face difficulties below ground as well. There is honey fungus. 'It's everywhere,' sighs Liz, 'but if I can keep plants healthy they're able to resist it.' There are plant-nibbling mice. 'I've seen tufts of plants disappearing down mouse-holes, or stood by a bed and heard them running along inside the walls.' And there are lawn-destroying badgers. 'I love them and don't want to exclude them, so I've now got a little electric fence I can put up temporarily to protect specific areas.'

Liz wrestles heroically with all these difficulties because she is passionate about plants. She is always trying new ones, often growing them from seed, saying, 'I'm driven as much by curiosity as anything.' Her garden doesn't have the 'one of this and one of that' feeling of many plant addicts' gardens, though, because her aim is to create whole communities of plants, which all live harmoniously together. She only intervenes 'when there are squabbles in the bed'. To that end, she works 'by trial and error, moving plants about until they're happy'. She is also willing to make frequent use of what she calls 'rogues and scallywags': plants which might become invasive elsewhere but don't in this difficult climate. Often, these are native plants or cultivated forms of them, such as

sweet woodruff (*Galium odoratum*), the variegated form of ground elder (*Aegopodium podagraria*), a pink form of campion (*Silene dioica*), a pale-flowered form of buttercup named *Ranunculus acris* 'Citrinus' or the form of celandine called *R. ficaria* 'Brazen Hussy'. She sometimes allows these to merge into the native vegetation at points she calls 'interfaces, places where you can hardly see what's garden and what's wild'.

Many more special and refined herbaceous plants are either skilfully knitted into this ground-covering carpet or given small specialized beds of their own where she can keep a discreet eye on them. Above the herbaceous plants rises a well-chosen selection of trees and shrubs, many of them unusual. Examples include an uncommon and elegant berberis, *B. dictyophylla*, which has pretty yellow flowers against small grey-green leaves, and an equally uncommon and elegant buddleja, *B. caryopteridifolia*, with delicate pale blue flowers and neat little leaves.

Liz has chosen many of the trees and shrubs because they extend the garden's season into late summer and autumn, which here is anything but one undifferentiated season. Leaf colour, for example, goes through so many stages that, Liz says, 'It's a bit like having

ABOVE The glory of autumn and the usefulness of contrasting foliage. From the left: tulip tree (*Liriodendron tulipifera*), *Buddleja globosa*, deciduous azalea, *Rhododendron yakushimanum* and *Acer palmatum* 'Atropurpureum'.

RIGHT Dewdrops on a red maple twig.

your own orchestral performance. The birches and aronias form the overture, then comes the symphony of rowans, maples and enkianthus, with the berberis and hydrangeas rounding things off.' She intensifies colour effects by careful positioning. 'I try to place plants with strong autumn colours so that adjacent plants provide a contrast of colour or a change of texture. So I put red maples next to matt-green rhododendrons, dark-leaved elderberry near yellow-leaved *Clethra alnifolia*.' Nor is autumn here just a matter of rich and varied leaf colour: there is also the richness of berry colour, from native and cultivated sorbus and from cotoneasters such as *C. salicifolius* 'Rothschildianus', *C.* × *suecicus* 'Coral Beauty' and *C. frigidus* 'Cornubia.'

Whenever Dick and Liz have one of their frequent informal 'Garden Open' days, they put a notice on the garden gate which announces the opening and includes a comment by a previous visitor:

Looking from the middle terrace of the garden to Hartsop Dodd, with *Rhododendron* 'Dusty Miller' in the foreground.

'You ought to be able to get a period of time in this garden on National Health prescription.' That visitor got it right. We would all be the better for regular doses of the Parcey House garden – not to mention doses of Liz Clark's passionate but unpretentious attitude to gardening.

There are no set times when the garden is open but if it is a fine day during the season the Clarks are likely to be in the garden, and if so the 'Garden Open' notice is likely to be up on the garden gate. Proceeds go to Diabetes UK. There is a car park at the eastern end of Hartsop but there is no parking on the village's narrow and winding 'main street'. A good alternative is to park at Cow Bridge, near Brotherswater, and then stroll up into the village.

Meconopsis 'Lingholm'

Ranunculus ficaria 'Brazen Hussy'

Corydalis elata

PLANT CHOICES

Some of Liz Clark's favourites.

1. Our garden has many daffodils. Most are cultivated forms, but we do have some of the wild one, *Narcissus pseudonarcissus*. I now wish I could get rid of all the 'tarts' and just have that simple beauty. It would suit me and my garden much better.
2. We have a number of *Rhododendron yakushimanum* hybrids but nothing quite matches the stunning species. This is sometimes recommended as a shrub for small gardens but our thirty-year-old specimen has had over 1,100 flowers in a season.
3. *Meconopsis* 'Lingholm' is reliably perennial and a lovely deep blue. I have steadily built up my stock and now have sufficient to carpet a little woodland glade. The astonishing sight always tempts visitors to come into the garden to see what it is.
4. *Euphorbia* 'Silver Swan' was a gift from the friend who discovered it. It has a wonderful statuesque form all year. It seems to be hardy, too, even in quite severe frosts.
5. *Ranunculus ficaria* 'Brazen Hussy' has dark leaves that set off the flowers admirably and is so tough it will even compete with the wild celandine. I like using plants which are closely related to natives: they fit and they thrive.
6. *Corydalis elata* is a really good-value plant. In February it carpets the ground with its rising cushions of soft green, fern-like leaves, above which the gorgeous blue flowers rise in early summer. There can be a bit of a messy period after flowering but if you cut everything down there's soon a new green mound, and a fresh crop of flowers in autumn.
7. The best camellia here is the old favourite *C.* × *williamsii* 'Donation'. It's well known for the best of reasons: it's good.
8. Not many visitors ever notice the golden woodrush (*Luzula sylvatica* 'Aurea') because there aren't many visitors around when it is strutting itself on a near-empty stage in January and February. Then it lights up the garden with its tousled golden leaves, which look especially attractive next to dark and mottled cyclamen leaves.
9. The astonishingly colourful foliage of *Aronia melanocarpa* heralds the autumn season here. It has become a real favourite of mine, yet it isn't a shrub you often see. There's the bonus of glistening black berries on mature specimens, too.
10. I love acers — any of them, except those closely related to sycamores — because they often have beautifully patterned bark as well as fine foliage. For example, I grew *A. davidii* from seed and it has now become a charming small tree, desirable both for its bark and for its autumn colour.
11. *Liquidambar styraciflua* is indispensable in autumn, because its leaves show so many different colours, from deepest purple to light yellow. They 'hold' well, too.
12. The scarlet oak (*Quercus coccinea*) is a more refined and less boisterous tree than the red oak. It colours up brilliantly in autumn but in our climate needs a sunny position. Mine get the shelter of nearby gold-leaved wild birches, which make a lovely contrast.

Grange Farm, North Cumbria

When Ian and Jane Gregg moved in the early 1990s to Grange Farm in rural north Cumbria, the charming early seventeenth-century farmhouse had 11 acres of land and 200 yards of river frontage but only a small 'farm garden' adjoining the house. Now they are the proud possessors of a garden ¾ acre in size, skilfully designed and atmospherically planted. Handsome drystone walls separate it from the surrounding fields and, while it forms a unified whole, it is clearly if informally divided into several different areas.

The garden's 'wholeness' comes from the way it is based on a striking and unusual combination of the very old and the very new. The old takes the form of the Greggs' interest in cottage gardening, vegetable gardening, wildlife gardening and organic gardening. The new is the garden's considerable population of contemporary abstract sculptures by two of their friends: Jake Harvey, who works mostly in stone and is Professor of Sculpture at Edinburgh College of Art; and Rob Harding, who lives in Spain and works mostly in metal. 'We think the combination of informal planting and abstract sculpture works amazingly well,' Jane comments. That is partly because the effect of a piece of sculpture isn't static but changes with the season, the state of the light and the time of day, so that even a single piece can substantially enrich a garden. An additional advantage of many of Rob Harding's sculptures is that sections of them are designed to move in the wind and as a result they subtly change shape. There is also one tall, totem-pole-like sculpture, with separate parts you can reconfigure yourself – making it 'something visiting grandchildren always love to play with'. Nor does sculpture just enrich the garden for humans. For example, *Oracle*, one of Jake Harvey's 'marker' series of sculptures, is positioned beside a pond, where it is much appreciated by fly-catchers as a launching post from which to swoop on their prey.

The success of this garden has been achieved despite considerable disadvantages. Because it is so close to the river its lower sections flood about twice a year, which means that to gather cabbages from the vegetable garden Ian and Jane sometimes have to wear waders and feel for them under water. Also the garden is north-facing, and so low lying that it is a frost pocket, with the last frosts sometimes as late as June and the first as early as

ABOVE Rob Harding's *Here to There* is the quirky focal point of the beds to the side of the house, in front of the sitting-out area.

RIGHT Looking down from the orchard to the courtyard and its dominating feature, the long multipart *Calanais* by Jake Harvey.

August. Finally, its soil is a light, free-draining loam, so ironically, although the garden is in a high-rainfall area and not infrequently flooded, the Greggs have to feed the soil heavily with moisture-retaining compost if plants – particularly vegetables – are to thrive.

The garden varies in design from relative formality to apparently complete (though in fact carefully managed) wildness.

The initial approach strikes a relatively formal note: you enter through a cobbled yard, once the farmyard, which is dominated by Jake Harvey's long and low but imposing *Calanais*, a homage to the famous circle of standing stones on the isle of Lewis. Immediately adjacent to the courtyard, however, is an ancient informal orchard of gnarled apple, plum and pear trees which Ian has skilfully pruned into new life. In spring the grass beneath their blossoming heads is thickly studded with wild flowers such as snowdrops, aconites, cowslips, bluebells and fritillaries. It also contains a scattering of tulips, whose cultivated formality is unexpected in such a cottagey context, but Ian explains, 'It just needed a bit of red to set off the other colours, and they were the ideal thing to provide it. I'm not a purist.'

The Greggs struggled for years to solve the difficulties of the areas alongside and immediately at the back of the house. Levels here changed awkwardly, while an old dividing wall and a covered-over farm tip further hindered coherence. Eventually they devised a subtle scheme of flowing 'informal formality' which united the whole area while providing a cobbled sitting-out place and a series of (mostly raised and stone-edged) beds. These house a collection of shrubs, many of them evergreen to provide winter structure (and shelter for the birds), underplanted with sturdy herbaceous favourites, such as hellebores, hostas, dicentras, geraniums, euphorbias, primroses and self-seeding foxgloves and poppies, all offset by some of Rob Harding's angular, bird-like zinc sculptures.

The lawn here gives an indication of further wildness to come. 'We used to cut it weekly, as a proper lawn, but now we only cut it every three or four weeks – and it's amazing how quickly things come back.' This semi-wild lawn soon modulates into a seriously wild (and wildflower) one around the garden's two artificial but convincingly natural-looking ponds. 'We sowed a wildflower-and-grass seed-mix on to the prepared soil,' says Ian. 'But I don't pretend this sort of miniature wildflower meadow is an easy thing to achieve. The undesirables always want to dominate.' The ponds are home to flourishing populations of frogs and newts, common and great crested. 'I've counted a hundred newts in an evening, so by now we may qualify as an SSSI.'

In the orchard in spring the fruit-tree blossom and bluebells, cowslips and tulips beneath the trees combine to produce an effect with the jewel-like richness of a medieval illuminated manuscript.

In the vegetable garden, formality is steadily swallowed up by abundant growth as the season progresses.

In this garden of something old, something new, the next section involves an appropriate 'something borrowed'. 'Reading Chris Baines's book on wildlife gardening twenty years ago transformed our whole approach,' Ian explains. 'We've borrowed many of his ideas – for example, in creating our miniature wood.' In it, native trees are underplanted with native wild flowers, while prunings are piled up to provide habitats for wildlife. There's another non-purist touch here, too: non-native buddlejas, 'for the butterflies'.

Beyond the beech hedge is Ian's no-dig vegetable garden, scrupulously maintained on a four-year rotation cycle. The rectangular brick-edged beds are enormously productive, thanks to every organic gardener's indispensable helper: a series of massive composting bins. The vegetable garden is also visually satisfying, particularly since the pattern of beds is enlivened by a series of tall metal 'tepees',

up which grow not only runner beans or sweet peas but also pumpkins and squashes. 'Pretty flowers, striking fruit and delicious to eat: what more could anyone want?' Ian comments.

His explanation of the vegetables he grows sums up the Greggs' attitude to gardening. 'I grow what the climate will allow, what I know will thrive here. We aim to enjoy the garden but not to let it dominate us. We've too many other things we want to do. So,' says this flood-plain gardener, with a wry smile, 'we don't try to push water up hill.'

The garden opens at least one weekend each year for wildlife charities and visits can also be arranged at other times. For information, email ian@grange-farm.org.uk.

Chard with winter frost

Squashes

Asparagus 'Franklin' F1

PLANT CHOICES

Ian and Jane Gregg suggest some native trees and vegetables for a damp cold site.

Native trees:

Among the native trees which have succeeded in our conditions are silver birch, elder, willow, hawthorn, blackthorn, field maple, beech, hornbeam, crab apple, dogwood, holly and yew.

Vegetables which do well here include:

1. We've found nothing to beat our favourite potato, 'King Edward'.
2. Among broad beans, 'Green Windsor' does well and is the nicest eater.
3. 'Painted Lady' is a very good runner bean and as well as tasting good it has pretty red and white flowers.
4. The best sprout here is 'Peer Gynt', but it finishes a bit early and we're still looking for a good late one.
5. The F1 hybrid asparagus 'Franklin' is great. We have two whole .beds of it.
6. We love purple sprouting broccoli. We grow an early and a late variety. They taste good and always look good in the garden, too.
7. And we love squashes. They're all delicious but our favourite is spaghetti squash. They're attractive from early July to late September. We cut them before the hard frosts, after which they become pieces of indoor sculpture while we eat our way through them. They usually last until March.

We get our seeds from Garden Organic (the working name of the Henry Doubleday Research Association), Ryton, Coventry CV8 3L8, telephone 024 7630 3517, website www.hdra.org.uk.

SCARTHWAITE, GRANGE-IN-BORROWDALE

The world's premier fern society, the British Pterodological Society, was founded in the Lake District and Borrowdale has always been the fern-enthusiasts' favourite haunt. So it is not surprising that there are hundreds of ferns in Nan Hicks' sophisticated ½ acre of cottage garden in the village of Grange at the head of Borrowdale, or that Nan is herself a devoted member of the BPS (the members of which she calls 'the Fernies' or, when she's feeling particularly irreverent, 'the Society of Fronds').

Scarthwaite was built in 1936 for Sam Hicks' grandmother and aunt, and his aunt passed it on to Sam and Nan soon after their marriage in 1959. When they arrived, the garden, says Nan, 'was either gravel or grass or rhubarb'. In the years since, it has, she adds, 'just Topsey-ed, as I nibbled away at the grass and planted in the gravel'. In the beginning, gravel and stones were pretty well all she had to work with: there was at best only the thinnest skim of soil over the rock. Over the years she has worked hard to build the soil level up with home-made compost, 'but most of it just gets washed away by our annual average of 120 inches of rain'. Even now, the ground is so stony that she can't dig here with a spade. 'I use my grandfather's old potato fork instead.' Preparation for a new plant has to be limited to 'excavating a hole for it and giving the hole a good lining of compost – after that, the plant's on its own'. The high level of rainfall means that her ancient *Osmunda regalis* flourishes even though it is planted in pure gravel. 'It must think it's in water,' chuckles Nan. 'It's a fern of very little brain.' But the stoniness also means good drainage, so plants don't become waterlogged.

Lack of soil and an excess of rain are not the only problems here. Wind frequently whistles up the valley from the south so strongly that, Nan says, 'In the early years, when the garden was less "wooded" and sheltered, I was once lifted off my feet and carried yards by it – and I'm no sylph!' So she has had to sacrifice much of what should be the garden's splendid views to create a miniature shelterbelt, mostly of junipers and rowans. 'If you leave gaps, you create wind tunnels, so now there are just glimpses of the views.'

The atmospheric approach to the house, swathed in densely planted garden and with the fells (High Spy and Maiden Moor) looming beyond. The large shrub by the door is *Viburnum × bodnantense* 'Dawn'. The pink blossoms beyond the bench are those of *Syringa × josiflexa* 'Bellicent'; *Sorbus aucuparia* is beside it.

ABOVE A 'moon opening' in the boundary hedge focuses the eye on the fell in the distance. It was made by Martin Roscamp, who lives just across the road from Nan. 'It's my favourite bit of the garden,' says Nan.

RIGHT The pergola in the 'new' area of the garden. Plants on the right-hand side include *Humulus lupulus* 'Aureus', rose 'Bobbie James', *Clematis* 'Multi Blue' and *C.* 'Paul Farges'. On the left is a beech hedge with various clematis growing through it. 'The sheep, despite all my efforts to prevent them,' says Nan, 'still succeed in pushing their noses through and attending to my pruning.'

The garden is also full of honey fungus. 'In the end, you just learn to live with it and avoid those plants which are most susceptible.'

Trees and big shrubs are not confined to the garden's boundaries. Nan has worked 'to have the whole garden feel like a wood'. And it certainly does, particularly the original part of it, which is wrapped tightly around the house. About twenty years ago, she and Sam acquired part of the adjacent field and that area, planted with hazels and fruit trees, is still rather more open – becoming steadily less so, though, as more and more plants sneak in. 'We actually lost quite a lot of trees there in the storm in January 2005 – not that anyone would notice. Indeed, nowadays, when something dies as a result of honey fungus, it comes as a bit of a relief. My planting style is based on sheer avarice,' Nan says, laughing, 'and the fact that I run an orphanage for other people's unwanted plants. I'm always finding little bundles on the doorstep.'

The main winding grass path is as narrow as possible, and, because of the density of shade, it is as much moss as grass. 'So I call it a green path, not a grass one!' Flanking it are shrubs for flowers (including rhododendrons, camellias, magnolias and osmanthus) and shrubs for berries (such as skimmias and the shrubby ivy *Hedera helix* f. *poetica*). The berrying shrubs are included partly to provide winter interest but also because this is a garden for wildlife as well as

wild plants: almost every shrub has its nest, red squirrels scamper overhead and hedgehogs hibernate in the cortaderia. Almost all also have, as Nan puts it, 'got a corset on' in the form of clematis or honeysuckle or both.

The underplanting is equally dense, but largely informal, squeezed into the gaps between shrubs and trees. Nan's many rare ferns are not confined to 'ghettoes' but are used here and there throughout the garden. Some appear as single specimens, in the ground or in pots (of every possible size and shape); others are used in drifts, among shrubs, among herbaceous plants, among spring bulbs, in walls and between paving stones. And every spare inch of ground is carpeted with woodland plants such as snowdrops, primulas, fritillaries, erythroniums, trilliums, uvularias and kirengeshomas. She grew many of her primulas from seed of an unusual Gallygaskins form (in which the sepals are enlarged to make a green collar around the flower). These have now spread into many-coloured drifts and are matched by drifts of snakeshead fritillaries which originally came from Margery Fish, with whom she used to correspond. Even where there is an occasional patch of planting which is both more 'structured' and more highly coloured — such as orange-flowered lilies rising through purple-foliaged *Lysimachia ciliata* 'Firecracker' — she is happy to let self-seeders infiltrate, if, like *Geranium phaeum*, they fit. Where there is no plant, there is an ornamental pot. There are even, lurking under a rhododendron, two lions by local potter Jane Smith. 'I call them my Dandy Lions.'

She sums up the garden's style by saying, 'I liken it to a drunken party — everyone leaning on everyone else.' Two small slate slabs, lying unobtrusively on paths at different points in the garden, underline her very personal approach. They have been inscribed — 'by our local tombstone-maker, now retired' — with quotations from her favourite garden magazine, *Hortus*. On one, a gnomic sentence by Adrian Fisher — very appropriate for this deliberately semi-wild garden — proclaims: 'I AM THE ANTIDOTE TO PLANNERS!' On the other is Tim Richardson's thought-provoking claim that 'WE SEE GARDENS NOT AS THEY ARE, BUT AS WE ARE'. Nan insists, though, that whoever sees Scarthwaite sees her. 'This garden,' she says firmly, 'is as I am.'

Having opened her garden for many years under the National Gardens Scheme, Nan is now scaling down her openings. She still opens occasionally for local charities and by appointment (telephone 01768 777233).

FOLLOWING PAGE Looking over Scarthwaite's miniature 'bog garden' towards the fell, Gate Crag, beyond. The large leaves in the foreground are those of *Rodgersia podophylla*, which is mixed with *Iris setosa*, *I. sibirica* and self-sown pink *Aquilegia vulgaris*. The tree on the right is *Sorbus aria* 'Hostii'.

Dryopteris affinis 'Cristata Angustata'

Adiantum aleuticum

Polystichum aculeatum

PLANT CHOICES

Nan Hicks enthuses about some of her garden's innumerable ferns.

1. Many *Polystichum* species have the advantage of looking beautiful even in winter. As a general rule, they are said to prefer lime in the soil, but those I grow seem quite content in my neutral-to-acid soil. They all insist, though, on good drainage. There are so many to choose from and all are beautiful. The North American western sword fern (*P. munitum*), for example, has splendid evergreen shuttlecocks of fronds. The hard shield fern (*P. aculeatum*) has deep green glossy fronds which look as though they have been varnished, while the fronds of *P. setiferum* 'Plumosum Bevis' have attractive, long-drawn-out, pointed tips.

2. The various forms of the hart's tongue fern (*Asplenium scolopendrium*) are equally useful in winter. *A.s.* 'Crispum Speciosum Moly' is a beauty, with goffered strap-like fronds about 40 centimetres long and up to 8 centimetres wide. Aspleniums prefer alkaline soil but will tolerate an acid soil provided it isn't too acid. It is best to grow them in shade because the fronds can burn in searing sunlight.

3. The members of the *Adiantum* genus look too fragile to grow in a windswept lakeland garden. They remind me of delicate scraps of green chiffon. Yet I grow several successfully. They don't seem to be fussy about soil but must have a sheltered tranquil nook in which to hide. *A. pedatum*, for instance, from the east coast of North America, is lovely but hates the wind. The Himalayan maidenhair *A. venustum* offers the bonus of often remaining green through the winter but, again, it must have shelter and shade. And I mustn't forget *A. aleuticum*, a maidenhair fern from the western coast of North America and Japan, which is one of the garden's star turns.

4. Not all ferns are evergreen. The *Athyrium* genus, for example, collapses in autumn. But its members are well worth growing for their delicate beauty in summer. The prettiest is the Japanese painted fern (*A. niponicum* var. *pictum*). Its fronds of pink, purple and grey look as though they have been washed with aluminium paint.

5. There are about 220 species of *Dryopteris* and many more hybrids. I wish I had room to grow them all. One of my favourites is *Dryopteris wallichiana*, which can grow up to 120 centimetres and looks as though it is covered in shaggy fur. *D. affinis* 'Cristata Angustata', a form of the native golden scaly male fern, is another good one. It has elegant narrow fronds, crested at the tip and down the outer edges, and stays green throughout the winter.

BRACKENBURN, MANESTY, BORROWDALE

From 1920 until his death in 1941, Brackenburn in Borrowdale was one of the several homes of the novelist Hugh Walpole. He described it as 'this enchanting place… this paradise on Catbells'. The enchantment for him lay in the views, both upwards to the fell behind and outwards and downwards to Derwentwater and the fells beyond. These it still has, but nowadays it has the additional enchantment of a fine garden, rescued, redesigned and replanted over the past two decades by Professor Derek Ellwood and his wife, Christine.

Out of necessity, the Ellwoods began with the hard landscaping. The steeply sloping site had once been terraced, but by the time they arrived much of the terracing had collapsed and had to be rebuilt. The same was true of the garden's drainage system – and drainage is vital in such a high-rainfall area and on a site overflowing with springs and streams. As Christine says, 'This will always be essentially a water garden – but you've got to get the water going where you want it to go, not where it wants to go.' This far inland and at this height (700 feet), there are two other significant factors that gardeners have to contend with: cold and wind. Cold winters limit the range of plants that can be grown, though Christine looks on the bright side by pointing out that cold also inhibits and delays the growth of weeds. Being in effect tucked into a cove, the garden doesn't suffer from continual strong winds, but it does suffer what is known locally as the Manesty Crack, a sudden blast of wind that rushes up the valley with what the Ellwoods describe as 'a sound like an approaching train' – often with damaging results.

When they arrived, the garden contained some fine structural specimens, such as 100-year-old examples of *Rhododendron arboreum* and *Acer palmatum* var. *dissectum*, but many other plants had got seriously out of hand. Bamboos, for example, had colonized rampantly while in a section below the house Portuguese laurels had grown so huge and ferns had spread so vigorously that it took the Ellwoods years to discover that they were hiding a rockery. They tackled the problem of overgrowth with a heavy-duty and still-continuing programme of pruning. 'It's the secret of keeping a garden like this

What Christine calls Brackenburn's 'unfair advantage': the spectacular view from the garden over Derwentwater.

under control,' says Christine. 'I always tell people, "Don't be frightened to use your secateurs."'

The rockery was not the garden's only hidden treasure: the Ellwoods also found abandoned statues scattered through the undergrowth. Some had suffered considerable damage. One is known as 'Frustrated Fred' because, as Christine puts it, 'We've never found his knees or bum.' As the figure has his hands over his ears, he's also sometimes known as 'LFA', for low-flying aircraft, which are all-too-frequent disturbers of the peace here.

There is a naturally good depth of acid soil almost throughout the garden (because of its high iron oxide content it looks oddly

ginger), but even so the Ellwoods continue to increase it by adding compost and leafmould. 'And now we buy lorryloads of chopped trees, which we feed with Growmore, and then add to the beds as well.' In the beginning, this acidic soil was something quite new to them, since previously they had done most of their gardening on dry chalk in Wiltshire. Beth Chatto's *The Damp Garden*, they say gratefully, became their bible.

As for an overall plan for the redesign and replanting of the garden, they insist that they didn't have one. The need to rebuild the terraces, add new ones, build steps to go with them and accommodate existing good plants, dictated the garden's design. Christine

LEFT The woodland with the beck pouring down from the slopes of Cat Bells above. The sides of the beck are carefully built up in stone because in wet weather, Christine says, 'It becomes a raging torrent.' The beck is criss-crossed with rustic wooden bridges and the paths beside it are richly planted, with rhododendrons, azaleas, hostas and ferns predominating.

RIGHT This little pool tucked in between the drive and a flight of steps is typical of Brackenburn's quirky charm and the way every corner holds something to catch the eye. The Ellwoods call this pool 'The Brothel'. Christine explains, 'It's where our frogs breed. The noise in spring is amazing. But in the past the tadpoles used not to develop. Frogs are important here – they're my slug-and-snail-killers – so now the tadpoles get rump steak every Saturday. Seriously! It seems to do the trick.'

says, 'We dealt with one area at a time and let the site itself tell us what was required. 'Accessibility' and 'nature' were our two ruling principles.' There was one other principle: to provide vistas – not big open views but glimpses, across, up and down the garden and out to the dramatic Borrowdale landscape beyond.

There is the same balance between formality and naturalness in the planting. As it has evolved, the garden has become increasingly one of carefully chosen and placed trees and shrubs set off by dense informal underplanting. Successful shrubs include of course rhododendrons and also magnolias, pieris, hydrangeas, skimmias, osmanthus and many *Camellia × williamsii* hybrids, while among the more notable trees are liriodendrons, halesias, embothriums, eucryphias, *Cornus nuttallii* and *Prunus × yedoensis*. But even if it is lovely, a tree that does not fit is removed. Recently a splendid *Pyrus salicifolia* 'Pendula' was taken out of the border beside the main lawn because its pruning required the use of high ladders and Christine says, 'Nowadays we're trying to make a garden for our old age.'

With the herbaceous underplanting, instead of indulging herself by planting as many beautiful individuals as possible, Christine uses fewer plants but in larger numbers. 'Planting in bold swathes and drifts is much more effective, as well as saving lots of energy.' The plants she uses are 'the traditional favourites for damp gardens – which are traditional favourites because they work' – hence the many ferns, hostas, astilbes, erythroniums, veratrums, rodgersias, epimediums and primulas.

The result of the Ellwoods' endeavours is a garden that suits its site perfectly, a garden of continually changing levels and points of view, in which dignified expanses of formal lawn or stone terrace alternate with steep slopes criss-crossed by winding flights of steps, while everywhere there are carefully channelled streams or cunning-ly created pools and dense but discriminating planting.

The garden opens each year for local charities from 2.00 p.m. to 5.00 p.m. on the last Sunday and Monday in May. Individual or group visits can be arranged at other times by appointment (telephone 01768 777200).

FOLLOWING PAGES
ABOVE This pair of topiarized 'twirls' stand at the top of a flight of steps and frame the view to the lake. They are probably part of the original 1905 planting of the garden.

BELOW A topiarized Scottish terrier stands guard on the main lawn.

Cornus nuttallii

Hydrangea paniculata 'Grandiflora'

Magnolia wilsonii

PLANT CHOICES

Christine and Derek Ellwood's selection of favourites, all of which do well in a watery hillside garden.

1. *Sarcococca confusa* is a small evergreen shrub with a neat habit. Its great season is in January, when its flowers produce a glorious perfume, like that of a bowl of hyacinths.
2. If you find that snowdrops do not like you, try snowflakes instead. We find that *Leucojum vernum* often does well where snow-drops do not.
3. *Prunus × yedoensis* makes a graceful small tree with arching branches which in early spring are covered in blush-white flowers. I love the way it has white flowers all along its branches, like ladies' bloomers.
4. The white bracts of *Cornus nuttallii* are a stunning sight in May and at the end of the season the tree also provides good autumn colour.
5. Our moist but well-drained acid soil is ideal for *Embothrium coccineum* and each May it rewards us with a display of spectacular red flowers.
6. *Syringa × josiflexa* 'Bellicent' is another fine May-flowering shrub. Its graceful racemes of pink flowers also lend themselves to flower arranging.
7. *Magnolia wilsonii* is an ideal hillside shrub, since it is best planted where you can look up into its pendulous white flowers.
8. We find that many of the species and varieties of *Epimedium* make extremely good — and also well-behaved — ground cover for shade and semi-shade.
9. *Hydrangea paniculata* 'Grandiflora' is a spectacular late summer shrub, with huge flowerheads. We cut it back annually to keep it to size and to encourage even more profuse flowering.
10. *Exochorda × macrantha* 'The Bride' is a wonderful shrub, covered in blossom from mid-May onwards for several weeks. It looks particularly good on a bank.

GREENCROFT HOUSE,
GREAT STRICKLAND

William and Maureen Irving arrived at Greencroft House in the village of Great Strickland near Penrith over thirty-five years ago. The acre or so of garden that went with it Maureen describes with grim simplicity as being then 'a jungle'. Part of it had been ploughed over during the war, planted with soft fruit and then abandoned, while what is now the large front lawn had recently been grazing for a farm bull. So the Irvings spent their first years endlessly cutting and pruning, clearing and digging. They had to deal with everything from entrenched perennial weeds to sizeable trees long past their sell-by date. They did not, they insist, begin with any clear idea of what the garden would look like when it was completed. Of necessity a 'garden of compartments', it has grown section by section as energy, inspiration and cash have permitted.

The solidly handsome house sits more or less in the middle of the flat site, and the garden wraps around it like a giant green muffler, protecting it from devastating winds. Maureen used to be an art teacher and her trained eye is apparent throughout the garden, both in colour combinations and in combinations of shapes, in small-scale incidents and in whole garden compartments. Indeed, rich variety is probably the garden's keynote, evident not only in its sophisticated use of contrasts and combinations of colours and shapes but also in the way the focus of the garden and the feeling it produces vary with the seasons. One section takes the starring role in the spring, another in the summer. Several even star in several seasons but with quite different plants and effects.

Often, adjoining sections of the garden are in completely different styles. One section close to the house, for example, is severely formal and geometric. It is simply a circular central bed within a square of hedging. In spring, the big circle, edged with clipped dwarf box, is often planted up with red tulips. In summer, when the tulips are over, it is densely carpeted with semi-hardy annuals. In both seasons, the effect is cool and restrained yet rich and satisfying. In contrast, just around the corner there is an area devoted to Maureen's beloved

OPPOSITE The upright shape of Charles Bray's millennium sculpture contrasts beautifully with the huge scalloped leaves of *Gunnera manicata*.

BELOW A study in contrasting shapes by the garden's lower pool: round hostas, upright irises and primulas, with clipped evergreens in the background.

alpines. Low, sloping and heavily gravelled, this rockery takes centre stage in spring with an explosion of jewelled, small-scale colour. For the rest of the year, it recedes into the background, yet it is never without interest, created by the sculptural effects of stone and gravel or skilfully placed plants with strong foliage.

Happy accidents and developments over time are something of a feature in this garden, as they tend to be in any good garden created over decades. A semi-formal vegetable garden, for instance, was originally designed to feed a family of hungrily growing youngsters. Now, since the youngsters have grown and flown, it has become an area where Maureen can try out new plants and plantings. In the same way, a gravelled drive to the side of the house became redundant as a drive but instead of simply languishing it has become a new garden compartment, containing transplanted specimens from Maureen's considerable collection of hostas. The area is ideal for them, since it gives them moisture at their feet, shade from the brightest midday sun but light overhead, and gravel around them to deter slugs and snails.

Although Greencroft House is surrounded by limestone, its soil is virtually neutral, so it suits almost any plant, particularly when boosted by regular additions of home-made compost. The garden is also rich in linked ponds and streamlets, and the planting around these is particularly impressive. From early spring onwards there are snowdrops, aconites and primulas of every size and style. These are followed by *Meconopsis*, many irises, and above all hostas. Maureen loves hostas for their texture as much as their colour; she has varieties with puckered, ribbed or smooth leaves. Then in summer the giant *Gunnera manicata*, like some elephantine rhubarb, looms up out of several corners. This is one of several plants which Maureen likes to repeat at different points through the garden. Because of the different contexts in which the plants appear, they produce subtly different effects yet help provide continuity. Another example of a repeated plant is the lovely spring-flowering Chinese shrub *Osmanthus delavayi*, which has deliciously scented little white flowers.

In spring, perhaps the outstanding plants in the garden are the hellebores, particularly innumerable varieties of *H. orientalis*, softly

rich swathes of which carpet many of the beds. In summer the same areas produce a quite different impression, the hellebores being largely swallowed up by a foaming sea of colour produced by plants such as poppies, thalictrums, campanulas and dianthus.

A complete catalogue of this garden would also have to include several areas which have been designed to create very specific effects: for example, the Gravel Garden, where imposing Cretan pithoi are placed among trees chosen for their tactile bark, and the purple and gold bed designed to display a series of contrasting foliage textures. Elaborate design and dense planting are this garden's hallmarks and even after almost forty years William and Maureen – aided by Agnes Chambers, whom Maureen gratefully describes as her 'knowledgeable and skilful gardener friend' – are still developing, refining and improving it.

The garden opens by appointment for specialist gardening societies or groups (telephone 01931 712236). In most years it also opens for a local charity or for the local branch of a national one.

BELOW The large central island bed in the largely red section of the garden Maureen calls the Borders Garden. The main plants here include the old double peony *P. officinalis*, *Primula pulverulenta*, *Allium aflatunense*, *Silene dioica* 'Flore Pleno', *Pyrethrum roseum*, *Astrantia* 'Norah Barlow' and *Thalictrum aquilegiifolium*.

FOLLOWING PAGE Hostas and *Primula japonica* sheltered from the sun by the giant leaves of *Gunnera manicata*.

Hosta 'Halcyon'

Glaucidium palmatum

Euphorbia myrsinites

PLANT CHOICES

Maureen Irving chooses plants to give a country garden both shape and colour.

1. Yew (*Taxus baccata*) is indispensable for giving a garden a framework and it's surprisingly quick-growing if well fed.
2. Trees that look good all year are another necessity. Three trusty favourites here are *Prunus serrula* (we sponge the bark each year to enhance its 'glow'), *Betula utilis* var. *jacquemontii*, with white bark which shines like a beacon, and *Acer griseum*, which is slow-growing but its peeling bark is so attractive that it's worth waiting for.
3. Hellebores, particularly *H. orientalis* hybrids, are wonderful for providing colour from December to April, a time when otherwise the garden would be quiet. They self-seed cheerfully, too, in a wide range of colours. When their season is over they have the good manners to take a polite back seat.
4. Foxgloves are ideal plants for a country garden. As well as the many forms of the native *Digitalis purpurea*, there are many other species worth trying. For example, *D.* × *mertonensis*, with flowers the colour of crushed strawberries, and *D. ferruginea*, which flowers in late summer with masses of tiny bronzey-orange flowers, much loved by bees and insects. We try to garden ecologically here so I'm always pleased when I find good plants which are also good for wildlife.
5. Almost all the many species of primula make perfect plants for damp Cumbrian gardens. The Candelabra primulas are my husband William's all-time favourites.
6. Hostas are my first love. I love their leaf form and the way they spiral into new growth. And they're so useful in so many ways in many different parts of the garden. I think it's hard to beat sturdy old-timers such as *H. sieboldiana* and *H.* 'Halcyon'. I'm less keen on the variegated forms, particularly those with white edges to their leaves. If we get a shower followed by sun, the white edges 'burn' and turn brown.
7. *Glaucidium palmatum* is a Japanese aristocrat, with handsome palmate leaves and large saucer-like lilac flowers for several weeks. Books say it needs shade but this far north I find it does much better in an open site, facing the sun, and in soil that is rich but well drained.
8. Meconopsis are great favourites here. I use them in just about every area of the garden and in every possible colour: lilacs, pinks, blues, yellows, whites.
9. The euphorbias are a fascinating genus, which provide architectural structure at a relatively low level. Particular favourites are *E. schillingii*, *E. myrsinites* and, even though it is not fully hardy here and sometimes gets cut to the ground in winter, the shrubby and scented *E. mellifera*.
10. Angels' fishing rods (*Dierama*) are lovely, graceful plants. In our climate they need to be in very well drained soil if they are to survive. Here, they grow virtually on rock – and are never fed. 'Blackbird' is a good, slightly darker form of the most commonly seen species *D. pulcherrimum*, while *D. igneum* is another good species to try.

DALEMAIN, PENRITH

Dalemain outside Penrith has been owned by the Hasell family for almost 350 years, during which the development of both house and garden has been typical of such sizeable but unpretentious Cumbrian properties. Changes have occurred in erratic bursts, as time, interest, energy and financial resources have allowed, and there has never been a complete reworking, of either house or garden. It is easy to see what Jane Hasell-McCosh, who now looks after the garden, means when she says, 'I'm often very much aware of being just one link in a very long chain.'

Like many other north Cumbrian country houses, Dalemain began life as a pele tower; it then grew first into a manor house and finally into a Georgian mansion. Similarly, what was originally a quite small utilitarian garden, devoted to fruit and vegetables, steadily expanded while becoming less and less utilitarian and more and more ornamental. As a result the 4 acres are rich with survivals of garden fashions from several centuries. There is a grotto from the sixteenth century, a knot garden and terrace walk from the seventeenth, and a summerhouse or gazebo (complete with its original painted seats) from the eighteenth. Even the garden's walls come from two different centuries: there is a seventeenth-century brick one and an eighteenth-century stone one. And from the nineteenth century there is a selection of fine mature trees typical of the period, including Britain's largest silver fir, *Abies cephalonica*, and, just as typical, a deep herbaceous border, running the full length of the terrace between the house and the deer-dotted eighteenth-century landscape park beyond.

LEFT AND ABOVE The knot garden. The fountain makes a classic centrepiece.

LEFT The house end of the long terrace border. The grey stone of house and outbuildings makes an ideal background for roses and an ivy.

BELOW Jane Hasell-McCosh is very much a hands-on working gardener. '*My* wheelbarrow,' she said firmly.

Dalemain is anything but typical, however, in the dominating role the women of the house have taken in the garden's development over the past two centuries. For example, Dorothea King, who married Edward Hasell in 1826, was responsible for the planting of trees such as the silver fir and for the creation of the terrace border. Among her successors, the next major contributor was Gertrude Hasell, a disciple of William Robinson, who in the early twentieth century introduced many of his gardening ideas to Dalemain, including areas of deliberately 'wild' planting and a much more relaxed style even in the more formal borders. That is very much the approach here still. 'Of course,' says Jane, 'we do have lots of plants which are clipped and shaped, but generally we try to get a relaxed and natural feel, with the planting hovering on the edge of being out of control. Rose Harper, who shares the work in the garden with me, once described the effect we aim at as looking as though the gardener had died about three weeks ago!'

Another major female influence on the garden was Jane's immediate predecessor, her mother-in-law, Sylvia McCosh. Her major innovation was to redesign the remaining working fruit and vegetable area, at the higher end of the upward-sloping walled garden, so that the whole became richly ornamental. She wisely retained gnarled old specimens of local apple trees but on one side of

them created a long border, backed by a wall and dominated by old-fashioned roses, while on the other side she replaced the soft fruit bushes with curving colour-themed mixed beds. Subsequently, she introduced into the informal woodland planting of the area below the walled garden, known as the Low Garden, bold stands of a richly coloured form of the perennial blue meconopsis, derived from plants originally given to her by its introducer, the plant-hunter George Sherriff. Her daughter-in-law comments, 'She was a real plantswoman and her garden was a real plantswoman's garden.'

Jane confesses that when she took over in 1991, she was not a gardener at all. She gratefully acknowledges that at first she learnt a lot from Liz Clark of Parcey House (see page 134). Then, by working together over the years, she and Rose have, she says, learnt and developed their own style. 'I'm very fortunate to have Rose, I know, because it's a great joy to work with someone so sympathetic, so much on the same wavelength.' She has tried to build on Sylvia McCosh's legacy, by adding more and more old-fashioned roses and more and more meconopsis. Also, 'I've tried to strengthen the beds' overall design. I work in combinations of plants, perhaps more than she did.'

Jane has also created completely new beds of her own. One of the most successful is known as the Animal Garden. When she first took over, her children were still young and often had to be in the garden with her while she was working. 'Since young children easily get bored in gardens, I had to find a way to entertain them, and get them involved. Because we had wormwood in the garden already and one of my children was interested in worms – as young children often are – I came up with the idea of creating a border full of plants with common names that involve creatures. So we had *horse*radish, *dog*wood, *goat*'s rue, *hedgehog* holly and the *ladybird* poppy, for example. And we tried to find ways to fit the plants together – or keep them apart – which were appropriate and amusing. So *cat*mint went close to the *mouse*plant but we kept the *fox*gloves well away from the *hounds'* tongues. And after a while we added to the fun by giving each plant a label in the shape of "its" animal. That part of the garden has become so popular that though our own children are almost grown up now, it's still there.'

Deer in the eighteenth-century landscape park.

Spectacular swathes in the Low Garden of Dalemain's fine form of the Himalayan blue poppy *Meconopsis grandis*.

Visitors certainly appreciate the results of these many generations of inspiration and hard work. 'It's become,' says Jane, with a slightly rueful laugh, 'the sort of garden visitors come back to again and again so that they almost feel they own it. Then of course they get their own ideas for how to develop it – and often they let you know what they are. They can be good ones, too. We once had a chap who wrote to ask for his money back he was so disappointed that the urns on the terrace weren't planted up. We'd never even thought of planting them but it was clearly such a good idea we've done it ever since.' Which is evidence that a large part of Dalemain's attraction today derives from its air of being not just steeped in history but also vigorously alive and looking to the future.

The garden is open daily from 10.30 a.m. to 5.00 p.m. from March to late October, and from 11.00 a.m. to 4.00 p.m. during the winter. Guided tours are available during the summer. There are plants for sale, including Dalemain's perennial blue poppy.

Symphytum × uplandicum

Solomon's seal (*Polygonatum biflorum*)

Rosa 'Roseraie de l'Haÿ'

Plant Choices

Jane Hasell-McCosh chooses a dozen favourites, some for sheer beauty, some for utility, some for both, and some also for their local or personal connections.

1. The Dalemain form of the Himalayan blue poppy (*Meconopsis grandis*) introduced by George Sherriff has to be top of my list. It's very much this garden's signature plant. What's more, its flowers are a wonderful colour, and it is reliably perennial.

2. My favourite plant in the whole garden is variegated comfrey (*Symphytum × uplandicum* 'Variegatum'). It's not invasive. (I wish it were: then I'd have made a fortune out of selling bits of it.) It's very early. And its luminous purple-blue flowers are stunning, particularly in late afternoon or evening light. If you cut it down when one flush of flowers comes to an end, it will go on and on right through summer.

3. On the terrace we've got that old favourite, St John's wort. All the *Hypericum* species are good but this one – I don't know its name – is a real toughie. It's always reassuring to find it going on year after year. What's more, my husband's colour-blind, so its bright yellow flowers are ideal for him.

4. This is a garden of roses and there are several I can't imagine it being without. 'Cerise Bouquet' is the first, because of its long flowering season, its elegant habit and its ability to cope with quite a lot of shade. The old China rose (now *R. × odorata* 'Pallida') starts flowering very early and sometimes goes on until Christmas, resists most diseases well and performs reliably even in poor, shallow soil. 'Roseraie de l'Haÿ' is indestructible, disease free, and with sumptuous plum-purple flowers, so good you want them to go on for ever.

5. Cardoon (*Cynara cardunculus*) is indispensable for its architectural grey foliage and imposing bulk. I cut the flowers off because the leaves are its real point.

6. Of the genus that used to be *Cimicifuga* and is now *Actaea*, I particularly love *A. simplex* Atropurpurea Group for its combination of height, handsome dark foliage and good white flowers in autumn.

7. *Brunnera macrophylla* 'Variegata', which we're now supposed to call 'Dawson's White', is an extremely effective foliage plant, though it has the disadvantage of always trying to revert. We split it each August.

8. The South African *Agapanthus africanus* has to overwinter in a greenhouse here but it's worth the trouble. My grandmother, Gertrude Hasell, who was South African, used to grow it, so for me it's a sort of memory of her.

9. The aconitums are fine and undervalued plants. They're far more valuable here than delphiniums, for example, since they cope with much more shade and don't break so easily in the wind. *A. napellus*, with purple and white hooded flowers, is particularly good.

10. No garden ought to be without dear old Solomon's seal (*Polygonatum biflorum*). It may be ordinary but it's still lovely. What's more, its elegant shape makes it perfect for flower arranging. I cut masses of it for the house. If you cut it down once it's finished flowering, you more or less eradicate caterpillars, which otherwise can strip the leaves in a day.

The Old Rectory, Dean

Although they take their gardening very seriously, Bill and June Wheeler of the Old Rectory at Dean near Cockermouth, on the northern fringes of the Lake District, don't take themselves too seriously. Making their garden involved, says Bill, 'what you might describe as a lot of creative tension'. That is hardly surprising, given that the two are passionate enthusiasts with slightly different enthusiasms. 'In the beginning, Bill planted too much too soon,' says June. 'He still does plant too much – and too close. He falls in love with things and buys them without thinking where they're going to go.' 'True,' he confesses, without looking the least bit guilty. 'June thinks in terms of colour. When her colour schemes come out right, it's because they're hers. When they come out wrong, it's because I've stuck in something I bought without thinking about where to put it or how it would look!'

When the Wheelers bought the property from the Church in 1988, both the house and its acre of garden needed considerable attention. The house had been battered by use as a Church Army headquarters, while the garden was reduced to the drive hedges, some mature trees, a few survivors from one rector's enthusiasm for roses and a lot of weeds. Given that Bill had just taken early retirement after a heart bypass, the place was a challenge. However, they knew they wanted to come back to the Lake District fringes, 'and this was much the best place we could find'.

Though they may disagree on details, the Wheelers are united about the garden's basic principles. Instead of a flat, blank, green, wind-swept canvas, what they wanted – and have created – was a sheltered garden of many different compartments. 'We didn't want everything to be visible at a single glance.' And they wanted to provide homes for many different kinds of plants and gardening styles, and a garden for all four seasons, relying as much on foliage colour and texture as on flowers.

They began work on the garden even while Bill and their naval architect son Guy were working on the house. They planted trees and hedges, changed levels to add visual interest, opened up the culverted beck which runs through the garden and added a terrace at the back of the house, known as 'the flight-deck' in honour of Guy's naval connections. Except for the paving stones for the terrace, the stone for all the walls and steps was found on site, and all the construction work was done by Bill and Guy. Meanwhile, June dealt with hundreds of cuttings, mostly of trees and shrubs, which they

OPPOSITE A wonderful piece of 'borrowed landscape': the honeysuckle-wreathed gateway through to the handsome church next door. The honeysuckle is *Lonicera periclymenum* 'Belgica'.

ABOVE The back of the house provides warm, sheltered conditions for climbers (such as the roses 'Lady Hillingdon', on the right, and 'Meg' on the left) and tender shrubs (such as a myrtle and a *Carpenteria californica*). In the centre, June's alpine bed. On the left, one of several island beds in this part of the garden.

had brought from their previous garden in Wiltshire. The garden's structural planting is based on those now-mature 'transplants'.

The Wheelers have clear likes and dislikes. For example, few of the compartment-producing hedges or the front edges of beds are straight because 'We like curves and contrasts.' There are no herbaceous borders as such, since 'We don't see the point of all that bare earth in winter.' And they use no annuals. 'Too much work!' A few specialist areas apart, such as the scree beds for June's beloved alpines, this is in effect a garden of mixed borders, with its many herbaceous plants and bulbs fleshing out a strong 'skeleton' of trees and shrubs. And it is designed to provide interest from the aconites in early spring to the autumn colours of acers and cornus.

Shortened at both ends and its straight sides disguised by broadly curving beds, the original long blank front lawn is hardly recognizable. At the house end, an entire section has been removed to create an appropriately dignified gravelled approach and turning semicircle, while the far end has become a cross between wildflower

meadow and miniature arboretum. Here a path mown through long grass full of daffodils, crocus, cowslips, fritillaries, ox-eye daisies, hawkbit and colchicums winds round a collection of fine specimen trees and shrubs. Similar specimens fill the bosomy beds down the right-hand side. Many are surprisingly tender, such as an *Indigofera* and an *Abelia schumannii*. Indeed, for a garden in inland north Cumbria the Old Rectory contains many surprising successes throughout, such as a *Carpenteria californica*, several *Leptospermum* and *Pittosporum* cultivars, an *Embothrium coccineum*, several different *Azara* and *Eucryphia* species, two mighty ozothamnus, and whole colonies of the Madeira orchid *Dactylorhiza foliosa*.

To the side of the house is a formal garden. Purple beech hedges bring out the light colours of its many roses, shrubby potentillas, dwarf hebes and, closing the vista and much loved by June, a pair of grey-leaved, blue-flowered *Perovskia atriplicifolia*. Below this area is a sunken garden, with a small pool, a rockery and a white border, including the lovely *Rosa pimpinellifolia* 'Dunwich'. Beyond, along the garden's boundary, lie several sizeable woodland sections full of rhododendrons, other shade-tolerant shrubs such as deutzias and many of June's small woodland treasures, such as trilliums, hellebores and erythroniums.

A rose pergola – which Bill describes ruefully as 'an exercise in controlled butchery' since it is planted not with climbers but

The pergola at the far end of the stone terrace is home to a selection of red- and white-flowered climbing roses, such as 'Madame Alfred Carrière', 'Sombreuil' and 'Altissimo'. Below them is the white shrub rose 'Boule de Neige'.

with rampant Rambler roses such as 'Treasure Trove' 'because they resist the wind' – forms a link between the woodland and the back lawn. That is broken up by island beds, including the scree bed, while a double border, in whites, yellows and blues, runs the length of the adjoining churchyard wall. The end of the border leads into a hidden cobbled courtyard, which provides shelter for semi-tender plants including a central *Buddleja alternifolia*, two vanilla-scented *Azara* species and, at the foot of a south-facing wall, a Californian tree poppy (*Romneya coulteri*). Finally, a rose-covered archway leads back to the front of the house and the end of the circuit.

The wise visitor, however, will immediately make it again in the opposite direction. This cleverly designed and densely planted garden has far too much of interest and beauty for it all to be absorbed on a single tour.

The garden opens by appointment under the National Gardens Scheme and is occasionally open for village and local charities. Garden enthusiasts are welcome to arrange a private visit (telephone 01946 861840).

Crinodendron hookerianum

Perovskia 'Blue Spire'

Anemone obtusiloba

PLANT CHOICES

Bill and June Wheeler suggest some good plants for every season from spring to winter and in every size from miniature ground-cover plants to sizeable trees.

1. Acers provide a wonderful variety of leaf form and colour. *A. palmatum* 'Sango-kaku' (aka 'Senkaki') has the added bonus of red winter shoots.

2. We're very fond of anemones. Two good spring-flowering species are *A. rivularis*, with large umbels of pure white flowers on long stalks, and the less frequently seen *A. obtusiloba*, with shorter stalks and smaller umbels and flowers in either white, yellow or deep blue.

3. Azaras are wonderful evergreen shrubs from Chile with vanilla-scented flowers from late winter through to spring. Both *A. microphylla* and the less hardy *A. lanceolata* grow successfully in sheltered corners here.

4. *Crinodendron hookerianum* is another Chilean evergreen, which does well here in shelter and shade. Its red lantern-like flowers are real eye-catchers for many weeks from late spring onwards.

5. We're very fond of daphnes. Late-winter-flowering *D. mezereum* f. *alba* and spring-into-summer-flowering *D. tangutica* are special favourites.

6. Erodiums are cousins of the geraniums and ideal for a rockery or scree garden. Most have fern-like foliage, while flower colour ranges from white or cream through to yellow and then maroon or magenta.

7. Primulas are a wonderfully versatile family, including plants of every size from rock-garden miniatures to 1 metre-tall giants for the bog garden. If we had to choose one, it would be that sturdy old favourite, the giant *P. florindae*, which self-seeds in damp ground throughout the garden and provides us with its wonderful scent and colours from pale yellow to ruby red.

8. Omphalodes are good sturdy ground-cover plants for shade and produce azure-blue forget-me-not-like flowers for long periods during spring. We particularly recommend *O. cappadocica* 'Cherry Ingram' and *O. nitida*.

9. We grow so many irises it's almost impossible to pick favourites, but if we had to choose just two we'd go for *I. chrysographes* 'Black Knight' for summer and *I. unguicularis* for winter – for its lavender or violet flowers and its delicious fragrance.

10. In a sunny well-drained spot, *Perovskia* 'Blue Spire', with its white stems, silver leaves and panicles of violet-blue flowers, takes some beating. It flowers for weeks on end in late summer and autumn.

11. Schizostylis covers the same period and seeds around in the drier parts of this garden. Deep red *S. coccinea* 'Major' is followed by pale pink *S. coccinea* 'Viscountess Byng' and then by the white *S. coccinea* f. *alba*.

12. *Sarcococca confusa* earns its place by the front door because of its wonderfully scented flowers for weeks in mid-winter.

FELLSIDE, MILLBECK

Clive Collins and his late wife acquired Fellside at Millbeck near Keswick in the mid-1960s almost by accident. Wanting a place from which they could easily indulge their hobby of fellwalking, they came to see another house lower down the slope, on the other side of the road, and as they came out after viewing it Clive looked up and said, 'That's the house I'd really like.' Although there was no 'For Sale' board, they were told that it was in fact for sale. 'So we went and saw it straight away.' They fell in love with the spectacular views across Derwentwater. The ferociously steep acre of garden was of no particular interest to them then. That is hardly surprising, since it consisted merely of a very 1960s planting of heathers in front of the house, a few rhododendrons above it and a vegetable patch sadistically placed right at the top of the whole plot.

Forty years later, the scene is very different. Fellside is now a densely planted shrub garden, a convincing mixture of Himalayan gorge, Tasmanian bush and North American forest edge. A mere acre it may be, but with its steepness, the corrugations in its slope (one including a delightful beck, masquerading as a Himalayan mountain stream) and the denseness of its planting, it feels like very much more.

To start with, the whole hillside had to be covered in a network of paths and terraces, to give both plants and humans a reasonable foothold. Nearer the house, the paths and steps are of Honister slate. It is impossible to use machinery here, so all the slate had to be hauled up manually by the two local brothers responsible for the building work, one of whom, John Allison, still helps today in the construction of wooden steps in the garden's upper reaches. Each year's leaf fall is gathered and then piled inside this wooden terracing and the leaves are left to rot down. Thirty-five years of such labour have produced an admirable depth and richness of soil. Understandably, Clive is somewhat miffed when visitors say, 'Of course, it's easy for you to grow shrubs here with such wonderful soil.'

Grow the shrubs certainly have, and in amazing quantities. The original few rhododendrons have become over 250, 150 of them wild species and many of those rare. There are twenty-five or more

Looking out from the end of the terrace, across the valley to the fells on the other side. The rhododendrons are red 'Elizabeth' in the foreground, 'Loderi King George' to the left, pink *R. orbiculare* to the right, a glimpse of yellow 'Crest' in the centre, and the tall slender pink *R. davidsonianum* thrusting skywards beyond.

FELLSIDE

different magnolias. There are two spectacular eucryphias which have grown to the height of a two-storey house and every year in late summer are smothered in thousands of white flowers. There are rare American cultivars of *Kalmia latifolia*, gifts from an American friend. Nowadays many of the shrubs have grown to such a considerable size that they have crowded out most of the underplanting, but Clive's daughter Melanie remembers that when she was growing up, 'There were actually lots of perennials too.'

It is in the nature of gardens – and gardeners – to change over time, of course, as Clive is keen to point out. With the years, he says with a smile, 'My taste has refined.' As a result, more recent plantings have consisted largely of rare species, such as the recently discovered *Rhododendron flinckii*, rather than showy cultivars. And many of his earlier plantings, such as a late-flowering rhododendron hybrid or a *Magnolia sprengeri*, which had been in position for more than fifteen years, have only recently become mature enough to flower extensively and make a real impact. 'You don't notice them for years and then suddenly for a time you hardly notice anything else.'

Though it contains many unusual plants, Fellside is anything but a random collection of 'specials'. 'I tried to plant by seasons,' says Clive. 'Early camellias led into rhododendrons and magnolias, then there were shrub roses for high summer, and eucryphias and hydrangeas for late summer into autumn.' However, he adds self-deprecatingly, 'I shouldn't have grown them all in mixed groups. Some just won't live together. The shrub roses, for instance, are always getting swallowed by the hydrangeas. If I were starting again, I'd certainly have more specialist areas, such as one devoted to the roses.'

If you pass along the shores of Derwentwater, particularly at any time from late April to late June, and look up towards Skiddaw, you may spot, at the upper limit of the houses scattered along its foothills, Fellside's multicoloured acre stretching up towards the skyline. Sadly, however, Clive has had to give it up. As he himself always insisted, change is indeed a part of gardening and at almost ninety he was finding the exceptional physical demands of this difficult site too much. So last year Fellside was sold and as yet no one knows what the future is likely to be for this remarkable garden. Whatever happens, at least Val Corbett's photographs will preserve it as it was in its maturity.

Following its sale, Fellside does not at the moment open to the public.

The gate at the bottom of the garden offers dramatic and enticing views upwards. The beck runs through the middle of this scene, though here it is invisible, lost under the layers of complex planting. The blood-red rhododendron in the foreground to the left of the gate is *R. campanulatum*.

PLANT CHOICES

Clive Collins makes a few general suggestions and particular recommendations, based on his forty years of experience of acid-loving shrubs.

1. Not many shrubs are equally distinguished in foliage and flower. If something has outstanding foliage it probably has fairly dull flowers and the other way round. *Rhododendron pachysanthum*, for example, has wonderful foliage. It keeps its previous year's leaves even when the new season's growth is advanced and the two seasons' leaves are quite different colours, both above and below, so you have four colours on a single shrub at the same time. On the other hand, it has unspectacular creamy flowers of no particular distinction. So you need to decide which for you is more important, foliage or flowers – or, if you want both, you need to select your specimens carefully, with some for foliage and some for flowers.
2. One of the rare shrubs that does have good foliage and good flowers is one that I consider the best of the many *R. yakushimanum* hybrids. Its name is 'Teddy Bear' and I recommend it highly.
3. In my experience, magnolias aren't as easy as books suggest. In their early years, particularly, they need attention. Give them shelter, talk to them, do anything and everything you can to make them feel loved and wanted. Then after a few years they become tough as anything and can be left to fend for themselves.
4. Camellias are much tougher and are available in greater variety than is generally appreciated. They are noble shrubs and if you give them a try you will not regret it.

MIREHOUSE, KESWICK

Mirehouse is special in two ways. Firstly because of its situation: it nestles on low ground close to the eastern shore of Bassenthwaite, with its own fells, Ullock Pike and Dodd (now leased to the Forestry Commission), rising dramatically behind it, and equally dramatic views in front across the lake to fells such as Barf on the far side. And secondly because of the close connections it and its nineteenth-century owners had with many of the great literary figures of the day.

Like many Cumbrian country houses, Mirehouse began as a simple farmhouse which was then gentrified and, like Topsy, just grew. An Earl of Derby in the seventeenth century began the process, which carried on when he sold the estate to his agent. Both the estate and its house remained in the agent's family until 1802, when its last representative left both to John Spedding of Armathwaite Hall. Spedding's descendant, John Fryer-Spedding, still owns and lives at Mirehouse today, together with his wife, Clare, their son James and his wife, Janaki.

It was that original John Spedding who began Mirehouse's career as a sort of literary salon. He had been a friend of William Wordsworth since their schooldays together at Hawkshead Grammar School and became close to Robert Southey after he became a neighbour at nearby Greta Hall. John's two sons also had literary friends. Thomas Carlyle visited Mirehouse several times at the invitation of his intimate friend Tom Spedding, after which he wrote nostalgically, 'Mirehouse was beautiful and so were the ways of it.' Meanwhile Tom's brother James's friends included Edward Fitzgerald (the translator of *The Rubáiyát of Omar Khayyám*), Arthur Hallam (whose early death inspired Alfred, Lord Tennyson to write *In Memoriam*) and Tennyson himself, who often stayed at Mirehouse and wrote many poems here, including much of *Morte d'Arthur*. Tennyson's Potting Shed, a recess in one wall of the walled garden, contains a copy of a drawing by James Spedding which shows the poet sitting in the recess, looking out gloomily while 'waiting for the rain to cease'. These writers loved Mirehouse both for the beauty of its situation (at least on days when it wasn't raining) and for the beauty of its garden.

The walled garden's summerhouse, seen through the blossom of one of the garden's many old local varieties of apple, probably 'Keswick Codling'.

Like the house, the garden's 20 acres have just grown; there was never a conscious overall plan. Ancient eighteenth-century Scotch pines still share the drive with huge nineteenth-century rhododendrons – hybrids, such as 'Grenadier' and pale-yellow-flowered 'Vienna', and large-leaved species, such as *R. falconeri*.

John inherited Mirehouse more than forty-five years ago from his distant cousin, Blanche, who had owned it for over seventy years. 'During all that time she never changed anything unless she had to – which had many benefits but some downsides,' John says. The main benefit was the preservation of much that deserved preserving. The main disadvantage was that nothing had been pruned or planted for decades. The shrubs on the drive, for instance, had been left for so long that they met overhead and formed a solid tunnel. And nothing had been done to replace old trees which were nearing the ends of their lives. Consequently, reclamation, replanting and simplifying so that the garden can be run with reduced modern labour levels have been major activities here for many years. Elaborate Victorian flowerbeds on the terraces in front of the house have been removed and the whole area laid to grass, into which wild flowers are allowed to infiltrate. The canopy of the woodland between house and lake has been thinned to encourage bluebells to provide a dense ground-covering and labour-saving carpet. 'I'm particularly keen on the plants of the forest floor,' says John. Even the thinnings were not wasted: they were piled against the fence to make a habitat for wildlife. In the same spirit, where he once planted exotics along the beckside walk known as Lovers' Lane, he now encourages native flowers.

The major simplified area is the 2-acre eighteenth-century Walled Garden, which is perhaps the most immediately eye-catching part of the whole garden. When the Fryer-Speddings arrived, it was still devoted to traditional vegetables, fruit and flowers. 'Full of bindweed. Impossible to keep up.' After several false starts, they arrived in the mid-1990s at the present labour-saving but visually satisfying arrangement. The original network of paths has been retained but the main focus of the garden is now on bees and their honey, so the garden is full of bee-friendly and nectar-rich plants. There are avenues of, for example, *Buddleja globosa*, *Eucryphia glutinosa* and a wide variety of ceanothus species and cultivars, which John praises as 'fine June-gap flowers for bees'. The bees are housed in the garden's bottom corner, their hives announced by their own giant name plate – a long but relatively

The house in its setting: looking back from the park to Mirehouse and the fells behind.

ABOVE John Fryer-Spedding's 'Folly', a circle of standing stones with a central circular stone table. It represents the Tennysonian Knights of the Round Table.

RIGHT The centre of the walled garden, with its geometric pattern of beds filled with low-growing herbs, and gravelled paths for ease of maintenance.

narrow piece of slate, into which is carved the first line of Virgil's fourth *Georgic*, which translates as 'First find a suitable site for your bees.' In another corner of the garden there is a miniature (and of course bee-friendly) heather 'path maze', 'not to get lost in but for meditation'. At the top of the garden is John's folly – 'Well, every garden should have one, don't you think?' – in the form of a circle of standing stones, 'mostly old stone gateposts from around the estate', with what was once a circular larder butter-stone acting as a table-top in its centre. The scene is intended to represent the Knights of the Round Table, in honour of Mirehouse's connection with Tennyson and his *Morte d'Arthur*.

John is particularly pleased that he and his wife have been able to renew Mirehouse's literary tradition by creating their own links with contemporary writers. Evidence of these can be seen on the rear wall of the fine rose-swathed Victorian colonnade, which is covered with the prize-winning entries in Mirehouse's annual poetry competition. It is no surprise that many of these prizewinners praise the beauties of Mirehouse just as fervently as Carlyle did.

The garden and the walks through the surrounding woodland and beside the lake are open throughout the season. For information, telephone 01768 772287, email info@mirehouse.com or visit www.mirehouse.com.

Buddleias form one of several avenues of 'bee-friendly' shrubs in
the walled garden: a simple, labour-saving but dramatic and
effective planting.

Rhododendron 'Songbird' with honey bee

Ceanothus thyrsiflorus 'Skylark'

Sedum spectabile 'Autumn Joy'

PLANT CHOICES

John Fryer-Spedding describes some favourites of the Mirehouse bees.

1. *Scilla siberica*. On a sunny day in February our *Scilla* bed is a mass of blue abuzz with early foragers for both pollen and nectar.
2. The *Ceanothus* family plug the June gap, especially for pollen production. Perhaps the favourite is *Ceanothus thyrsiflorus*.
3. Our herb garden is stocked with favourites of the bees. Especially popular are chives (*Allium schoenoprasum*) and borage (*Borago officinalis*).
4. A favourite vegetable is the leek (*Allium ampeloprasum* subsp. *porrum*), if allowed to flower, in August and September.
5. The loudest buzzer amongst the fruit is the raspberry (*Rubus ideaus*). And a good buzz is prophetic of a heavy crop to come.
6. Of the shrubs, the yellow *Buddleja globosa* gives long service. If deadheaded, it flowers from August until November. The eucryphias, especially *E.* × *nymansensis* and *E. glutinosa*, are invaluable for autumn forage after the heather is finished.
7. On the Mirehouse buzzergraph *Cotoneaster horizontalis* (flowering in July) tops the chart for wall plants.
8. *Sedum spectabile* 'Autumn Joy' is a good nectar producer from September to November.
9. The dwarf *Rhododendron* 'Songbird' produces deep blue flowers in April and September which are ever popular among the bees for their abundance of (clean) nectar.

Cautleya spicata

WINDERWATH,
TEMPLE SOWERBY

Winderwath near Temple Sowerby in the Eden Valley is a mature Victorian country house garden, with the sort of laid-back charm characteristic of that period. However, restoration and renewed planting over recent years have made it also a Mecca for plant enthusiasts. Whole areas are now full of rarities, all of them interesting, many of them beautiful, and most of them grown from seed acquired by owner Jane Pollock and head gardener Ron Davies from sources all over the globe.

The oldest parts of the house date back to its fifteenth-century origins as a small manor house and it remained largely unchanged throughout succeeding centuries, when many similar houses were given stylistic 'makeovers' by almost each new generation. It was only in the middle of the nineteenth century that its then owner, a local builder who aimed to turn himself into a country gentleman, gave it the hefty extensions which make its present façade so imposing. The 5 or 6 acres of kitchen and ornamental gardens were presumably laid out at the same time, though it is not known who designed them; certainly the mature trees that are a feature of the garden today, including wellingtonia, cedar, and beeches both cut-leaf and copper (*Fagus sylvatica* var. *heterophylla* and *F.s.* Atropurpurea Group), are very much trees of that period. In front of the house a main vista was created down a terraced lawn to an ornamental pond, with more informal areas of ornamental woodland on either side, while the kitchen garden (still lovingly maintained) was tucked in alongside the house. The Victorian builder's attempt at gentrification had a sad end when his only son was killed in a boating accident and in despair he sold up. After that the house had several further owners before being bought by Jane Pollock's parents in 1947.

Barbara Pollock was a keen gardener and David Pollock a keen forester. He planted trees and shrubs which enriched an already well-endowed garden and his legacy can be seen today in mature specimens such as a swamp cypress (*Taxodium distichum*), an autumn-colouring *Stewartia pseudocamellia* beside the pond and an

Arisaema ciliatum

Cardiocrinum giganteum var. *yunnanense*

OPPOSITE Dieramas from South Africa flourish in the warm shelter and good drainage of this bed flanking the path into the garden.

Acer griseum with spectacular peeling bark. She specialized in alpines, creating rockeries and planting up a series of red sandstone troughs.

Jane Pollock had nothing to do with the garden until after her mother's death in the mid-1990s. 'We'd only have argued over it,' she says with a smile. Then, together with Ron Davies, the head gardener who has been here for nearly twenty years, she set about reclaiming abandoned areas and expanding into new ones. 'We didn't have any great schemes for major changes,' Jane says. 'Just tinkerings and fine tunings.' These included clearing the pond and lushly planting its edges with drifts of primulas, while a bridge has been built over the ditch to make a complete circuit possible. Also, over recent winters Ron has rebuilt the main sandstone retaining wall across the lawn, incorporating into it a seat for people and troughs for plants, and creating above it a splendid new rockery bed. 'Years ago,' he says gleefully, 'I'd have died for a rockery like this.' The wonderfully gnarled and weathered pieces of limestone incorporated in the bed's surface were discovered when the old wall

was taken down: they had been used as filling-in material behind the wall. 'They must have come from an abandoned Victorian rockery,' says Jane. 'And just look at them,' adds Ron Davies, 'positively begging to be planted up. They're like little gardens in themselves.' Already the bed is filling with treasures such as several unusual daphne species, quite tender ginger relatives from the *Roscoea* genus, and the supposedly impossible *Iris orchioides*, one of the seed-grown rarities which Ron somehow persuades to flower here in the open every year.

In many ways, Winderwath is an unusually favourable spot for growing such plants. Only 300 feet up and sheltered by trees, it is in a slight rain shadow, so it is much less wet than many Cumbrian gardens. Except around the pond, its soil is light, sandy and free-draining. As a result in the sunniest and most well-drained spots such unlikely exotic delights as South African nerines, eucomis and dieramas (angels' fishing rods) flourish. 'I had romantic dreams of the angels' fishing rods nodding gracefully above the waters of the

pond,' Ron comments ruefully. 'But it was just too damp down there. They had to come up on the terrace.'

Winderwath offers plenty of proof of the old gardening adage that every positive has its negative. Its mature trees, for instance, offer shelter but also mean dry shade and root-infested soil. Even so, Ron Davies has had some remarkable successes in extending even his 'exotic' planting into such conditions. For example, many of his favourite unusual salvia species have coped there surprisingly well. The hardier ones come from China and the Far East, including *S. hians*, *S. bulleyana*, *S. nilotica* and the big bold *S. przewalskii* with mauve-purple flowers. 'Books describe that one as disappointing,' he says incredulously. 'Nonsense! It's a gem.' Many of the more tender South American species also often survive here over winter in the ground, though Ron employs the sensible insurance policy of cuttings, taken late and kept under glass.

He is fascinated by salvias, as he is by roscoeas, arisaemas and innumerable other genera, partly because he is an enthusiast and

ABOVE Wonderful contrasts of form and foliage in the mature woodland fringes of the garden.

FOLLOWING PAGE The dense planting around the edges of the pond includes swathes of self-seeded primulas.

loves the challenge of something out of the ordinary. But his fascination also has a practical purpose. 'When you open to the public, you're always thinking, "What comes next?" And of course it is hard to find things which flower towards the end of the season. The salvias are wonderful in that respect. Some years they go on flowering here until December.' Certainly, in whichever of its nine months of opening each year you visit this atmospheric garden, you can be sure that there will always be plenty to see.

The garden opens from 1 March to 31 October, on Monday to Friday from 10.00 a.m to 4.00 pm, and on Saturday 9.00 a.m. to noon. There are always plants for sale, many of them unusual and all grown on the spot.

Philadelphus 'Belle Etoile'

Mosla dianthera

Salvia involucrata

PLANT CHOICES

Head gardener Ron Davies selects a few particularly good plants from Winderwath's wide range, including some that are rare.

1. I am not a galanthophile: my favourite spring plant is not the snowdrop but the humble winter aconite (*Eranthis hyemalis*). The huge drifts here of its cheerful yellow blooms fill me with the joy of spring.

2. I am fascinated by the *Arisaema* genus and grow dozens of different species, both little and large. My favourite is *A. tortuosum* var. *helleborifolium*, grown years ago from seed collected by Chris Chadwell. Its wonderful if intimidating chocolate-brown stem rises to over 1 metre and its green spathe has a tip that extends so far that it seems to defy gravity.

3. I grow many *Roscoea* species successfully here. My favourite is *R. alpina*, which grows to about 12 centimetres, has deep purple flowers and is worthy of a place in any rock garden.

4. Of all the ginger family, *Cautleya spicata* holds a special place in my affections. I grew it from seed many years ago. It has proved perfectly hardy here and its flowers always add a touch of the exotic before winter sets in.

5. The daddy of all the plants I've grown from seed must be *Cardiocrinum giganteum*, if only because it took eleven years from seed to flowering. And even better than the type, in my opinion, is *C.g.* var. *yunnanense*, which is slightly smaller — though even so up to 2 metres or more tall — with brown stems and enormous white purple-flushed trumpet-shaped flowers.

6. My favourite rose is another seed-grown plant. *Rosa brunonii* is fairly rampant and its savage thorns make it a pruner's nightmare, but despite that I wouldn't be without it. It produces huge quantities of its white flowers and they have a perfume to die for.

7. Many years ago, on holiday in Fishguard, I spotted *Salvia involucrata* at a nursery and had to have one. I still grow descendants of it today, and out of the more than forty salvia species and varieties I grow here, this is still the best. It makes a proudly erect plant with purplish green leaves and a profusion of wonderful beetroot-red flowers from late summer until the first frosts.

8. Philadelphus are a delight — to look at, to smell, and even to look after and maintain. 'Belle Etoile' seems to me to epitomize all the good points of the genus.

9. My final choice will be unknown to many gardeners. I originally grew it under the name *Mosla grosseserrulata* but now I think it is actually *M. dianthera*. Whatever its name, it is an extremely good plant, with sternly attractive leaves and deep powder-blue spires of bloom in autumn. It is one of those plants that everyone wants as soon as they see it.

Acorn Bank, Temple Sowerby

The garden at Acorn Bank in the Eden Valley looks as old as the venerable house it surrounds. In fact most of it was created less than a century ago by a remarkable woman, Dorothy Clough (1888–1967), by nom de plume Dorothy Una Ratcliffe and by respectful shorthand simply DUR. She was the author of dozens of plays, books of poems, books of stories and books about her travels. She was physically imposing – unusually tall, with a wild crinkly mane of hair, a great beak of a nose and a mouthful of skewed horsey teeth – and her character matched her appearance: she dominated just about everyone she met by her total conviction that she knew best about absolutely everything.

DUR spent the happiest years of her life with her second husband, Noel McGrigor Phillips, at Acorn Bank, which she acquired in 1934. The restoration of the house and its grounds was their shared project, the symbol of their love. After her husband's sudden death in 1943, Acorn Bank never meant as much to her, and by 1950 she had decided to hand it over to the National Trust.

The history of the site goes back at least to the Knights Templar, who had a religious house here in the thirteenth century. What DUR acquired, however, was a handsome but dilapidated nine-bay red sandstone house, an eighteenth-century adaptation and updating of buildings from the previous two centuries. She immediately set about restoring it, but she did so very respectfully, sprucing up the Jacobean panelling and the eighteenth-century plasterwork, and adding some contemporary but sympathetic oak doors by 'the mouse man', Robert Thompson of Kilburn.

Outside she was much more ruthless and remodelled rather than merely restored: changing the layout, revising and enriching the planting, and adding many impressive decorative embellishments, such as statuary and some fine ornamental ironwork gates. By using 'picturesque' planting within a largely existing framework, she aimed to increase Acorn Bank's 'antique' atmosphere. It was a sort of con trick, but a sophisticated, civilized, sympathetic and successful one.

The centre of the redesigned Herb Garden: still informative but now much more open, spacious and visually attractive.

The Walled Garden, for example, she transformed from a working garden into an ornamental area, while retaining elements of its recent past – and even of its more distant past, when it was part of the life of a religious house. She also created the Sunken Garden, which has recently been restored to its original appearance using evidence provided by old photographs.

In spring, the many old local apple varieties in DUR's sizeable orchard, with evocative names such as 'Lemon Square' and 'Lady's Finger of Lancaster', are laden with blossom, while the grass at their feet is studded with wild flowers. In autumn, there is of course the attraction of the varied colours and shapes of the apples themselves, which are at their best for Acorn Bank's annual (and much loved and anticipated) Apple Day. The long mixed borders at the foot of the orchard walls are a fine sight at any time from late spring to late summer. These were replanted a few years ago and are lovingly maintained by gardener Chris Braithwaite and a team of volunteers. Chris forms a double-act at Acorn Bank with his wife, Sarah, who is the custodian of the house and of the property as a whole.

Away from the more formal areas adjacent to the house, DUR turned the surrounding oak woodland into a picturesque wild garden by increasing the existing native plants and adding many others, in particular great drifts of daffodils (even if not quite as many as her whimsical description of herself as 'the Lady of a Million Daffodils' would suggest). It is characteristic of her unscholarly imagination that many of the daffodils she planted were not in fact wild species but unusual cultivated varieties bred by Backhouse of York. Since many of those varieties are now very rare, they make a springtime visit to the Acorn Bank woodland fascinating for daffodil enthusiasts.

Perhaps DUR's most significant legacy to the Acorn Bank garden was to begin again, in a small way, the tradition of growing herbs. She assumed that there had been herbs growing here in the house's early days, though Chris Braithwaite is a bit doubtful about that. 'Most supposedly old formal herb gardens in this country turn out to have been invented by Edwardian ladies.' In the 1960s DUR's tentative beginnings were greatly extended and formalized by

Graham Stuart Thomas, and Acorn Bank's Herb Garden became the largest collection of medicinal and culinary herbs in the north.

By 2000, however, his scheme, with its narrow paths, straight-edged beds and big blocks of plants, was in need of revision. Chris's inspiration for a new design was the ancient botanic garden at Padua, which is divided into four quarters and then intricately subdivided, so that 'the overall effect is nice and twirly'. Wider paths were needed for wheelchair access, and that, Chris says, 'gave us the chance to revise the whole layout'. Now the paths have 'passing places' in bays inset into the beds and a more open central area. Those changes inspired changes to the layout of the plants as well, 'so that it makes more aesthetic and intellectual sense': it is now in triangles, 'two sizes of triangle, for different sizes of plants'. Why the triangles? 'Because they interlock so nicely. Originally I thought of clipping all the shrubs into triangles, too, but perhaps that's going a bit too far.' And the plants are now organized into groups according to their functions. The four beds in the centre, for example, are devoted respectively to plants for 'heart', 'head', 'love'

OPPOSITE There are seductive changes of level as you look up from the recently restored Sunken Garden to the border along the upper wall of the orchard.

ABOVE This newt-rich pool is the centrepiece of the restored Sunken Garden.

FOLLOWING PAGE The orchard in autumn.

and 'stress'. Chris points out proudly that even in high summer the whole area, though by then lush and leafily abundant, remains visually attractive and coherent.

Acorn Bank is not a showy place. Unlike its original creator, it doesn't seek to dominate, impress or astonish. What it does do, though, is charm, and that it does very powerfully.

The garden and grounds at Acorn Bank are open Wednesdays to Sundays throughout the season until the end of October. The grounds are also open during March for snowdrops and early daffodils. There is a Newt Watch in the Sunken Garden in spring and an Apple Day in the middle of October. For details of these and other events, telephone the Acorn Bank shop (01768 361893).

Astrantia maxima

Eryngium alpinum, one of the sea hollies

Selinum wallichianum

PLANT CHOICES

Chris Braithwaite cunningly chooses not so much plants as a whole plant family.

I'm very fond of all the members of that under-appreciated family, the umbellifers. (I know we're now supposed to call the family *Apiaceae* but they're still umbellifers as far as I'm concerned.)

To start with, they're a varied family and offer a wide range of very different attractions. Some are useful economically, because they're edible – carrots and parsley, for example. Others, such as hemlock, water dropwort and giant hogweed, are interesting – to me, at least – because they're dangerous. Many of them are also very decorative, with fine architectural foliage. And that foliage comes in many different styles, from the featheriness of fennel or the *Selinum* species to the sword-like leaves of the sea hollies. As those two examples prove, umbellifers also come in many different sizes, from low sprawlers to back-of-the-border giants. It's true that they don't offer many different flower colours, but they have flowers in fascinating shapes – the flowers of the astrantias, for example. I particularly love the way the flowers of many of them – such as those of fennel – are like a sort of dome floating on top of almost nothing.

Of all the umbellifers, though, my favourite, because it is both decorative and useful, is that simple old-fashioned herb, dill.

CHAPELSIDE, MUNGRISDALE

At Chapelside in the fell village of Mungrisdale over three decades Tricia and Robin Acland have created a garden that is a sophisticated but playful combination of her sweeping drifts of classic country garden plants and his 'fabrications' – the name Robin gives to his sculptural artefacts made out of found and recycled materials. That recycling illustrates another important aspect of the Aclands' style: a concern for the environment. The garden is organic and wildlife is welcomed or, as in the case of destructively digging badgers, at least tolerated, while its design echoes and eventually merges into the spectacular landscape around it.

When the Aclands arrived in the mid-1970s, the house had only recently stopped being the heart of a small mixed farm. The L-shaped range of house and barns was probably built in the late eighteenth century. The small areas of garden by the house all had severely straight stone walls, to keep out stock, and there was much buried concrete flooring from destroyed outbuildings. First this had to be removed and then quantities of additional soil were brought in. Partly because that soil was of varying quality and kinds, conditions in different parts of the garden have proved to be equally varied. And as always, fine views mean foul winds, so getting trees and shrubs to establish here is never easy or quick.

Over the years the Aclands have removed straight lines and straight walls to create a flowing garden not of 'rooms' but of areas, each with its own distinct atmosphere. The garden first snakes around house and outbuildings and then leads outwards and upwards towards the fellside. In Robin's self-deprecating phrase, it is 'more tricksy' near the house and becomes consciously wilder in its further reaches, until eventually 'it merges back into the hill'.

The bed beside the barn to the right of the house houses many plants for late summer, while the focus of the adjacent lawn is one of the garden's imposing sculptures, a fibreglass piece called *Sails* by local sculptor James Reynolds. The south-facing bed directly in front of the house is a gravel garden for plants that appreciate its heat and good drainage. These include alliums, cistus, *Iris unguicularis*, a bronze phormium, *Asphodeline lutea* and a selection of ornamental grasses. The bed also acts as a home for one of Robin's own sculptures, a circular four-part concrete piece, like the petals of a gigantic fading flower or a disintegrating boat, jokingly called *Instant Relic*.

Spring light across the new pond, with framing trees, daffodils and the 'borrowed landscape' of the fell beyond.

LEFT The house tucked in at the foot of the fell and its driveway, now flanked by the garden.

RIGHT, ABOVE The square bed by the entrance gate – here with tulips, meconopsis and trollius – is at its most colourful in spring.

RIGHT, BELOW The stone river.

On the other side of the drive, the original straight-walled kitchen garden has long been removed and its site given over to a combination of lawn and steadily expanding curved beds which overflow with a profusion of roses, cirsiums, eryngiums and geraniums, their colours mostly blue, maroon, purple and white. A flight of drystone steps, hand built by Robin with treads that are mainly huge old roofing slates, leads to a gravelled terrace in which sit mighty boulders (dropped in by JCB from the neighbouring field), while on the further side of the terrace an outbuilding has been converted into a handsome summer room. Another old farm outbuilding has also been converted into a split-level gallery for changing displays of more 'fabrications'. The building was once a forge and the Aclands still call it the Forge. Why? 'Because it contains forgeries!'

Skirting to the left of the house you come to some of the most remarkable of Robin's outdoor works. First is the Fernery, a stone-walled pit, appropriately damp and cool. This was originally given four vertical sides, but then the Aclands found a frog trapped in its depths, unable to scale the stony cliffs, and as a result it now has one elegantly sloping side – a perfect frog exit. Adjoining the Fernery is a stone river, a bed perhaps 3 metres long by 1 metre wide, in which slate slivers embedded narrow-end-up suggest watery currents surging past miniature but still substantial boulders, its elegant sculptural simplicity reminiscent of ancient Japanese gardens.

That area leads through to a vegetable-plot-cum-cutting-garden. The beds here are formal in shape but the planting is exuberant. Beyond that again lies the wilder garden, where a tiny stream has been opened out into an artificial but natural-looking pond of considerable size. Even without artificial aids, this is almost always remarkably clear, 'because the water comes straight off the fell and is continually moving through it'. When weed does occur, it is removed by someone paddling over the surface in a coracle Tricia made for the purpose.

As the ground gradually rises towards the fell, the garden becomes less and less garden and more and more fell. In the centre here is a meadow area, planted for succession with fritillaries, pheasant's eye narcissus, camassias, ox-eye daisies and yellow rattle (*Rhinanthus minor*). Finally, around the top of the garden runs a narrow shelter belt. At one point the path which meanders through it is enlivened by *The Crocodile's Wigwam*, a sculpture Robin made 'out of last year's cornus prunings'. These wooden pieces, of course, disintegrate over time, 'but that's part of the fun'. Another example runs along the boundary drystone wall – his *Wall-Wide Web*. Here twigs, arranged in interlocking waves, are battered each winter by the westerlies, and then renewed, the sculpture thus remaining the same yet different.

From that highest point, the path winds back down towards the house. After a while, there is a seat from which to contemplate the whole scene, tucked in among scattered damsons and a miniature

grove of six white-stemmed *Betula utilis* var. *jacquemontii*. Then the path skirts an older and much smaller pond, home to frogs, toads, palmate newts – and a crocodile. Safely inanimate, this monster, lurking in deep shade, was made out of driftwood from an Argyll beach. The edges of the pond also provide perfect homes for hostas, primulas and tricyrtis. Below that is the gravelled entrance drive, beside which is the garden's most recent addition, a crevice bed in which large stones, deeply sunk on their edges, provide a cool root run for alpines. The drive itself is half-covered with *Primula florindae* and irises, 'mostly yellows with the occasional dash of white', which are allowed to spread wherever they want.

One of the main beds in summer, with eryngium, *Knautia macedonica* and geraniums, the composition held together by mounds of golden marjoram and silvery stachys.

That sort of 'going with the flow', plus Robin's notion of the garden as 'a place in which there should be some room for fun', perfectly summarizes the engaging approach behind this original and delightful garden.

Chapelside opens under the National Gardens Scheme and by appointment (telephone 01768 779672).

Anemone trullifolia

Geranium 'Ann Folkard'

Oemleria cerasiformis

PLANT CHOICES

Tricia Acland chooses her favourites from spring through to autumn.

1. *Oemleria cerasiformis* is one of the first shrubs to break into leaf. Its light green leaves sit along the branches like little shuttle-cocks, beneath which appear pendent racemes of white scented flowers. It is about 2 metres by 1.5 metres.

2. Spring-flowering *Sanguisorba canadensis* 'Plena' has delicate white flowers packed with narrow petals. Scalloped greyish leaves outlast the flowers and are very attractive. It needs leafmould and part shade.

3. We grow *Camassia leichtlinii* 'Caerulea' in grass along with pheasant's eye narcissus to follow *Fritillaria meleagris*. It has 1-metre spires of starry blue flowers in May. The white form is also lovely and flowers a little later.

4. Tiny *Anemone trullifolia* 'Alba' flowers profusely in early summer and then intermittently well into autumn, with dusk-blue buds and open, white, gold-centred flowers with blue reverses. It needs fertile, not too dry soil and sun or part shade.

5. Grown in a border, fennel (*Foeniculum vulgare*) provides easy architectural structure and a filmy texture from early spring through to autumn. The bronze form, *F.v.* 'Purpureum', more commonly grown in borders, offers different 'combination' possibilities.

6. *Geranium* 'Ann Folkard' sends out 1 metre-long stems, with the result that the magenta flowers pop up unexpectedly through other plants. 'Patricia' is similar, as is 'Anne Thomson' (though she is smaller and has golden foliage).

7. Finally a selection of plants that make the most of a gleam of sunlight and show up well against our drystone walls: a ribbon of *Milium effusum* 'Aureum' through a spring bed; clumps of *Luzula sylvatica* in damp shade or woodland edge; a border edging of golden marjoram (*Origanum vulgare* 'Aureum') and silvery *Stachys byzantina*; for low winter sun, orange or pinkish grasses such as *Stipa arundinacea*.

BEAUHILL, PENRITH

Dr Hugh Barr and his wife Margaret have lived on Beacon Edge above Penrith since 1953. Their house, Beauhill, is part of the Victorian spread of substantial sandstone villas on to the flanks of the long arching hill in the shelter of which the original Penrith settlement was formed. Miles from the sea, 700 feet up, only 40 miles from the Scottish border, and completely exposed to winds from the south, east and west, it hardly seems at first sight the dream location for a gardener with a keen interest in growing plants from Australasia. Yet Beauhill has two great natural advantages: it faces almost due south, and its steep slope means that water and cold tend to drain away quickly. And over the years Hugh has built up a third help to a gardener in this situation: what was originally open hillside is now thickly planted with a considerable array of substantial trees, attractive in themselves and providing vital shelter against cutting winds.

Because of the steepness of the slope and the thickness of the tree planting, the garden is one of continually changing levels and little sheltered nooks and corners. Each of these has its own microclimate: some are sunny; some are shady; some have rich moist soil; others have soil that is poor and stony; and some have virtually no soil at all, merely naked rock, in the cracks and crevices of which suitable plants somehow find a toehold. The different levels are linked by winding paths and narrow and precipitous flights of stone steps, which are unnervingly slippery after rain. Everywhere there are eye-catching rarities, because Hugh is a serious and distinguished plantsman, but the overall effect is eye-catching too, because the whole garden has been designed so that it fits into the rugged landscape.

Beauhill has a remarkable range of the larger and showier Australasian trees and shrubs, with good examples of hoheria, eucryphia, callistemon, grevillea, clianthus, corokia, leptospermum, olearia and pittosporum. The main focus, however, is on plants that are less often seen because they are smaller or quieter or, quite often, both. Shrubs of that sort, in which Hugh takes particular pleasure, include coprosmas and species of what used to

Although the garden is 700 feet up in inland north Cumbria, this palm tree, *Trachycarpus fortunei*, seems perfectly happy, protected by the steps from the back door up to the main garden.

be *Hymenanthera* and are now *Melicytus*, both grown largely for their berries. Other interesting smaller Australasian shrubs grown as much for their foliage as their flowers include daisy-flowered *Pachystegia insignis*, which has dark green leaves with striking white-felted undersides, the dense rounded bun of *Brachyglottis spedenii*, and, at the lowest level, quirky little alpine hebes such as *H. buchananii* and seldom-seen *H. haastii*.

Not all Beauhill's southern hemisphere foliage plants are shrubs. Among the largest herbaceous plants, for instance, are astelias and dianellas, mostly with big, bold leaves, something like those of a phormium. Libertias create a similar effect on a slightly smaller scale, particularly *L. peregrinans* and *L. ixioides*. Substantially stiffer than the foliage of the libertias, and sometimes almost as large and imposing as that of the dianellas and astelias, is that of Beauhill's

fascinating collection of spiky-leaved aciphyllas. These have mostly been grown from seed, most of which (like that which has produced many other plants here) has come directly from New Zealand: from the New Zealand Alpine Garden Society, from botanic gardens and from specialist commercial collectors. Another group of plants Hugh uses for their evergreen foliage are southern hemisphere grasses and their relatives. Their most spectacular representatives are the New Zealand grass trees, the dracophyllums. *D. milliganii*, for instance, has made trunks up to around 3 feet in height, topped by a ferocious-looking rosette of broad, stiff, spiky leaves. The effect of a well-placed group in one of the garden's miniature woodland dells is bizarre and dramatic.

Beauhill's Australasian bill-topper, however, is its remarkable collection of *Celmisia* species and naturally occurring hybrids –

'They're very promiscuous,' Hugh says with a sigh. But he often says of a particular specimen that it may be a hybrid but it is 'a very nice plant, all the same' (being a true Scotsman, 'very nice' is about as effusive as he gets). He adds, 'People do so like to have names. I sometimes think they care more about the names than they do about the plants.' All the many species of *Celmisia* (and those accidental hybrids) have attractive daisy flowers and evergreen (though in fact often silvery) leaves, arranged in rosettes which vary in size from dinner plate to egg cup. To thrive they need rich soil, maximum drainage, plenty of light and sun, and shelter from damaging winds, all of which this expert plantsman has cunningly contrived for them.

This multitude of Australasians – as well as many others from other parts of the world, such as Mexico and Uruguay – succeeds

OPPOSITE A typical corner of this densely planted garden, full of unusual specimens. On the left is a dramatic clump of giant phormium foliage; at the back, a wonderful place to sit out, with swags of the mauve-purple flowers of *Wisteria macrobotrys* cascading downwards.

ABOVE A winding path snakes between informal but cleverly judged planting, full of contrasts in shapes and colours. In the left foreground there is an impressive clump of *Astelia nervosa* 'Red Gem'.

here against the apparent odds because a discriminating and enthusiastic gardener has chosen and positioned them wisely. As a result, Beauhill is a hugely inspiring place to visit.

The garden opens for small groups or for individuals by appointment. Telephone 01768 862913.

Parts of the garden produce the effect of miniature exotic, almost alpine meadows.
The star turn here is *Bulbinella angustifolia* with its yellow flower spikes.

Celmisia sessiliflora

Weldenia candida

Paraquilegia anemonoides

PLANT CHOICES

Hugh Barr's selection combines big structural plants and miniature beauties.

1. Without Japanese maples this garden would be bare. They and the rhododendrons, which grow well in the sandy soil, form its 'skeleton'. Of course skeletons tend to be forgotten, but they shouldn't be. And the maples are interesting to grow from seed, even when the seed requires stratification. Occasionally one is surprised by one that germinates like mustard and cress.

2. *Eucryphia* × *nymansensis* is a fine tree, though not one that is easy to please in a garden as dry as this. I try to avoid using a hosepipe so, in periods of drought such as the one we had in the summer of 2005, I carry buckets of rainwater to it from my various barrels.

3. My first interest was in alpines. As far as I am concerned, these include woodland plants – and woodlanders seem to like the conditions in this garden, perhaps because of the good drainage. Particular favourites include a trio from North America: *Trillium grandiflorum* (there are also many other desirable species); *Galax urceolata*, a pretty but slow-growing ground-cover plant with many milky white flowers in spring and leathery leaves that turn bronze or red in autumn; and *Sanguinaria canadensis* – the double form is very desirable and fits into any small corner that offers leafy soil and shade.

4. *Weldenia candida* from Guatemala is a beauty. Its three-petalled, pristine white flowers each last only about a day but production continues for quite a time and you can increase the effect by building up a little *Weldenia* colony. I find it difficult to gather seed of it but it is easy to propagate by cuttings. I have it planted on a slight slope, in sandy soil with added leafmould. In that situation it seems quite hardy, though I cover it in really wet spells.

5. *Paraquilegia anemonoides*, which has finely cut foliage and pretty bowl-shaped lilac flowers containing a striking central 'bush' of yellow stamens, is a fine plant for a rock garden that is well worth growing even though it needs cross-fertilization to set seed. Use a suitable paintbrush to achieve this. Once you've got seed, you'll find that it germinates well.

6. *Physoplexis comosa*, with fascinating bottle-shaped flowers, is a nice plant for a trough. It needs full sun and sharp drainage, and, since it comes from a limestone area around Monte Baldo in northern Italy, it appreciates having some Dolomitic lime added to its compost.

7. I wouldn't be without bulbs in the garden. Two favourites are *Galanthus* 'Sam Arnott' and *Fritillaria meleagris*.

8. A couple of good twiners that will grow through shrubs without becoming a nuisance are *Codonopsis convolvulacea* and *Tropaeolum tricolor*. The only disadvantage with the *Codonopsis* is that after producing its lovely flowers it dies back completely, so over-keen weeders can easily remove its small tuber by mistake.

HUTTON-IN-THE-FOREST, SKELTON, NEAR PENRITH

The origins of Hutton-in-the-Forest, like those of many of the large houses in north Cumbria, go back to a pele tower built for defence against marauding Scots. The garden at Hutton today, however, is essentially a palimpsest of life here since the mid-seventeenth century. Every few generations there was a change of taste, a surge of interest or a sudden influx of cash – and as a result significant changes. None of those changes, though, ever completely obliterated what was here before. As a result, the gardens, like the house for which they provide a fitting setting, are historically fascinating as well as atmospheric and beautiful.

The earliest detailed record of the garden at Hutton is an early eighteenth-century Kip engraving, which shows a grandiose Restoration layout in the Dutch style, with imposing terraces on the south and west sides of the house and enormous vistas through trees planted in rows like soldiers on parade. Only a few years after the engraving was published, though, that formality began to be softened. More fine trees were added, such as oak, beech and lime, and increasingly they were chosen and placed as much for their beauty as specimens as for their part in a formal scheme. Ponds (the largest of which, covering 4 acres, might well be called a lake) and a cascade were created in the woodland, partly to produce fish but also to produce an aesthetic effect. What had previously been a 2-acre formal and completely open garden to the north of the house was walled on two sides to provide shelter for fruit trees and, perhaps, for more purely decorative planting.

In the early nineteenth century, at around the same time that Salvin was Gothicizing the house, Sawrey Gilpin was called in to advise on making the garden more Picturesque. Towards the century's end the area to the south, once home to those formal vistas, became the Low Garden, its planting dominated by fashionable Victorian conifers and rhododendrons, and elaborately topiarized yew hedges were added to enclose the other two

'Masses of lovely colour' in the Walled Garden from (among others) red poppies, pale purple *Hesperis matronalis*, yellow alchemilla, the blue flowers of *Cynoglossum* and the blue foliage of *Hosta sieboldiana*. The tall spikes towards the back are *Eremurus robustus*.

sides of the garden to the north, now a kitchen garden but also including some flowers.

All of which explains why, if you ask the present Lord Inglewood how large the garden is, his answer is, 'How long is a piece of string?' That is, it depends on where you think of 'the garden' as ending. As he points out, in the seventeenth century, when the formal vistas went on into the parkland beyond, 'This wasn't Versailles but it was moving in that direction.' For most people nowadays, though, 'the garden' is really the area immediately adjacent to the house – though even this covers something like 20 acres. In Richard Inglewood's downplayed description, these acres constitute 'a garden of several bits'. The seventeenth-century terraces to the south and west, now in their nineteenth-century dress (complete with strange topiary shapes at one end of the south terrace), still command splendid views. Nowadays, though, the

views are of the undulating 'foliage tapestry' of mature eighteenth- and nineteenth-century tree plantings. The Victorian Low Garden retains its layout of paths in the shape of two interlocking stars, which provide their own miniature picturesque vistas, and contains many fine individual specimens. (Hutton's tree planting tradition has been continued by Richard's father and now by Richard himself.) Sadly, though, most of the hybrid rhododendrons in the Low Garden have reverted to *R. ponticum*, but at least its flowers make impressive banks of pinky-mauve each June.

For most people, the most immediately eye-catching part of the garden at Hutton is the 2 acres or so of the Walled Garden. 'This is Cressida's world,' says Richard firmly. 'I know nothing about this sort of gardening.' As late as the 1950s, the Walled Garden was still a partly functional area, a mixture of flowers and vegetables; Richard's parents grew flowers commercially there to send to

Looking towards the north side of the house across the hedges and topiary shapes of the Walled Garden, with peonies in the foreground.

market at Covent Garden. It is the present Lady Inglewood who over the past twenty years has made it what it is today, though she points out how fortunate she has been in her inheritance. To start with, 'The trees and the pink-grey stone of the house make a wonderful backdrop, I think.' Then there is the eighteenth-century layout, by which two cross-paths divide the whole area into quarters, and the 'outer skeleton' of eighteenth-century brick walls and nineteenth-century yew hedges.

Within that formal outline, Cressida's intention has been, she says, 'above all, to create somewhere relaxed and peaceful. I don't want weeds but I don't want a garden filled with plant-labels, either.' Her main priority is 'masses of lovely colour'. And that is how the borders here are organized: in terms of their colours. Not, usually, single colours (though one quarter in late summer becomes almost a 'white garden') but combinations of them. As you enter the garden

Dramatic contrasts of colour and shape in the Walled Garden. The tulips include 'Ballerina', 'West Point','Orange Emperor' and 'Uncle Tom'.

from the south terrace, for example, the borders nearest to you are in blues, whites and yellows. In summer they overflow with 'masses' of white geraniums and polemoniums, tall white and blue campanulas, tall blue and yellow aconitums and the foaming heads of *Aruncus dioicus*, all pierced by the bold verticals of teasels and *Eremurus himalaicus*. Supporting Cressida's statement that 'We plant what is happy here, so there is a mixture of the ordinary and the unusual', one of these borders also contains *Clematis recta*, treated as a herbaceous border plant by being supported in a 'cage' of beech twigs. 'It's a lovely plant but a demon to train,' is the heartfelt comment of gardener Di Howard.

Cressida insists that the garden is very much a partnership between her and Di. 'We discuss things all the time, pointing out to each other what's working well and what needs attention.' They both agree that getting roses to perform satisfactorily here is not easy. 'Richard's father used to say that,' Cressida remembers. 'In the beginning I thought, "I'll show him!" But now I know he was right.' 'It's so sheltered in here,' Di adds. 'I think that's why it's difficult to

keep them healthy.' As an example of something not working, Cressida points out a dramatic sea of purple-blue *G.* × *magnificum*: 'Though I'm a geranium fan, I have to admit it has rather got out of hand and needs to be reduced.'

This 'spirit of revision' has been typical of Hutton for centuries and continues today. At the moment, for example, Richard is contemplating clearing the *R. ponticum* from the Low Garden and felling selected trees in order to restore the original vistas; once again these would meet in the distance beyond the main pond-cum-lake, which would be dredged and 'resized'. 'At the meeting point,' he adds wryly, 'ideally there ought to be an eye-catcher – a temple or something of the sort – but that's only likely to happen if I win the Lottery.'

The garden is open from 11.00 a.m. to 5.00 p.m. from 1 April to 29 October (except on Saturdays). There is a numbered list available of the main trees in the woodland. The house is also regularly open and when it is so is the tea room. For more information, telephone 01768 484449 or visit www.hutton-in-the-forest.co.uk.

Thalictrum species

Rosa 'Paul's Himalayan Musk'

Melianthus major

PLANT CHOICES

Lord and Lady Inglewood and their head gardener, Di Howard, each make a 'mini-selection' of some of their favourites.

Richard Inglewood's favourite trees:

1. Spanish chestnut (*Castanea sativa*): I love the leaves, both their shape and their autumn colour, and the spiral bark. Sadly, Spanish chestnuts don't grow as well in Cumbria as I would like. I suspect our veteran example is the oldest tree here, possibly dating from the seventeenth century.

2. Large-leaved lime (*Tilia platyphyllos*), which Henry Fletcher included in a series of avenues he planted here in the mid-eighteenth century. In its heyday it must have been a very spectacular scheme but sadly many of them have blown down during my lifetime.

3. In my view the cedar of Lebanon (*Cedrus libani*) is probably the finest conifer there is, greatly superior to the Atlantic cedar. It also has an exotic and historic resonance, of course. Unfortunately, the one at Hutton is not an especially good specimen.

4. The massive pole of the Lowes fir (*Abies concolor* Lowiana Group) was the tallest tree at Hutton and, possibly, briefly the tallest tree of its type in the UK. It was then 48 metres high, but now the top has died back.

Cressida Inglewood's favourite flowers:

1. Every year I think how miraculous is the way snowdrops come up and give us clouds of their beautiful pure flowers for more than a month through the worst of the weather. I'm particularly fond of the simple single ones.

2. The clusters of small delicate pink flowers of the rose 'Paul's Himalayan Musk' provide a brief but glorious sight on a south wall of the house in late June.

3. *Melianthus major* is indispensable because of its elegant grey-green architectural foliage.

4. I first saw whole fields of cosmos growing wild in Mexico and have loved them ever since.

Di Howard's favourite flowers:

1. I admire *Lathyrus odoratus* 'Matucana' for its richness of colour and scent in summer.

2. I admire *Maianthemum racemosum* (formerly *Smilacina racemosa*) for its strong form and its abundance of creamy flowers.

3. I admire almost all the thalictrums for their delicate foliage, pretty flowers and sturdy self-supporting stems.

4. I admire *Actaea simplex* 'Brunette' for its fine foliage, its late flowers and the challenge of getting it to grow well.

NUNWICK HALL, GREAT SALKELD

Nunwick Hall at Great Salkeld near Penrith is a Victorian country house still lived in by the family for whom it was built and run entirely as a family home. The Thompsons, a Liverpool banking family, bought the Nunwick estate in 1889 and immediately substituted a new house for the handsome part-seventeenth-century Old Hall. (They had the good sense not to demolish the Old Hall, which is still used as additional accommodation today.) Then they went on to lay out new gardens around the house. The Thompsons have been an impressively long-lived family: the fourth generation took over only eight years ago, 120 years after the family purchased the estate. The original purchaser, Richard Heywood Thompson, was succeeded by his nephew, Colonel Cecil Thompson, he by his sons Walter, Oliver and Martin, and they by Martin's son Myles, who lives here now with his wife Jo and their young children.

Gardening at Nunwick is not without problems. Only a spade's depth down is pure sand. As a result the soil has to be incessantly fed. Even so, plants grow very slowly and Stephen Busbridge,

LEFT The summerhouse at the end of the great lawn is surrounded by deep beds including many tall upright plants – required if the beds are to make an impact in such a large space – and the even taller uprights of occasional sculptures.

BELOW In the right light, the red Lazonby sandstone of the house has a lovely soft glow. Between the upper terrace and the lawn are the recently rebuilt and extended terraced beds, made from the same fine local stone.

one of two full-time gardeners and head gardener since 1988, says bitterly that in the kitchen garden replacement apple trees have hardly bulked up after ten years. Another problem is relatively low rainfall, at least in Cumbrian terms, which, in combination with the sandy soil, means that after even a few rainless weeks watering becomes a necessity. 'We save every scrap of rainwater,' explains Jo, 'and now we've even sunk a bore hole.' Then there is the savage north-easterly known as the Helm Wind, which frequently howls down from the heights of Cross Fell and batters the garden. As if that weren't enough, although Nunwick is in a frost pocket it rarely gets enough snow to act as a protective plant-cover.

The 6-acre garden is a fascinating mixture of traditional and modern. 'I'm trying to give a modern spin to a Victorian garden,' is how Jo puts it. Adjacent to the house is its most formal section, a grand terrace and, continuing beyond the house frontage, what was originally an enormous herbaceous border. Family tradition records this as having been, when it was created in the 1890s, as long as the deck of the biggest ocean liner of the day. Like much of the rest of

the garden, over the years it has been modified to cope with changes in taste and reduced staffing levels. Recently it has been redesigned as a double rather than single border. Into its Jekyllian swathes of traditional country house plants Jo has inserted occasional large, quirky pieces of modern sculpture, 'all by young and up-and-coming people'. Then the mood modulates, via a formal low-walled square with a central pool, into a small wildflower meadow, beyond which fields lead the eye to the skyline fells.

Below the terrace and herbaceous border, the ornamental garden becomes more informal. There are three particularly eye-catching features. The first is a small sunken area, its charming fussiness suggesting perhaps Edwardian rather than Victorian origins, surrounded by handsomely shaped yews and entered down steps under a yew arch, with a fine Coalbrookdale seat at its far end and an even finer metalwork pergola in its centre.

The second feature, undeniably Victorian and grand, is ½ acre of sunken rock garden made out of enormous rocks. Typically for the time, these were laid with no attention at all to the alignment of strata.

In the twenty-first century such a rock garden is both a privilege and a nightmare to possess, a rare and potentially beautiful survival but extremely labour intensive. When planted, it is unreachable by machines, so all weeding has to be done by hand. For that reason, until a few years ago it was partially filled in to make it manageable. Recently, however, the filling-in has been removed, with exciting results – in particular, the discovery of a forgotten central pool crossed by gigantic stepping stones. And in the latest and most ambitious move this mighty rock garden has even been extended. Jo explains that the intention – 'once we've got rid of the twitch' – is to replant it all as a fernery, interspersed with occasional dwarf azaleas and self-seeding primulas and foxgloves.

The third feature in this part of the garden is an imposing lawn created below the terrace by Cecil and Rachel Thompson. From the 1930s onwards, they gradually removed the existing clutter of Victorian shrubberies and winding paths in order to make a single impressive (and more easily managed) green expanse. At its far side, however, there is a single swirling bed, which Jo has recently

Decorative as well as useful: the central herb section in the Walled Garden, with bronze fennel *Foeniculum vulgare* 'Purpureum' in the foreground.

extended and planted mostly with ornamental grasses, from among which peek several more pieces of modern sculpture. These are much smaller than those in the herbaceous border, 'so that I can move them around as the grasses grow up'.

Finally, there are Nunwick's 2 acres of walled kitchen garden. It is rare and heart-warming to see a working garden of this size so lovingly maintained to such high standards. The garden still has sections devoted to traditional vegetable growing, soft fruit, flowers for cutting and the production of all the herbaceous and bedding plants for the main garden. Here, too, though, there have been sensible modifications to cope with modern conditions. Herbs are grown decoratively in a small formal potager surrounded by 'hot' borders and the two ends of the garden, surplus to practical requirements, have been turned respectively into an ornamental orchard, where free-range chickens roam, and a splendid laburnum walk.

Nunwick is not the sort of garden which dazzles with showy design or rare plants. Instead, it is a place of relaxed stylishness, comfort, far-sighted common sense, hard work and old-fashioned levels of skilled cultivation. An eye-catching modern sculpture of a giant fork surmounted by a butterfly emerging from the Edwardian abundance of a herbaceous border, twenty-first-century children's plastic toys beneath a magnificent Victorian conifer: such pictures epitomize the charm of this quintessentially English country garden and its combination of 'ancient and modern'.

The garden opens for different charities each year and private group tours can be arranged by appointment. For more information, telephone 01768 881205.

The peaceful, cool calm of the Sunken Garden makes a refreshing contrast to the drama of much of the rest of the garden.

Penstemon species

Cowslip (*Primula veris*)

Love-in-a-mist (*Nigella damascena*)

PLANT CHOICES

Jo Thompson and head gardener Stephen Busbridge each choose half a dozen of their favourite plants.

Jo Thompson's choices:

1. I have loved cowslips (*Primula veris*) since I was a child, so I'm delighted that we now have some growing successfully in our newly created wildflower meadow.

2. Penstemons provide a wide and lovely range of plant sizes and flower colours, and the flowers last well into the autumn.

3. Foxgloves are another of my childhood favourites. Our daughter is named after the Welsh word for foxglove, Ffion. So I'm delighted that more unusual varieties are becoming increasingly available.

4. The wedding cake tree (*Cornus controversa* 'Variegata'), with its layered branches, bright green leaves with creamy-white margins and pretty clusters of white flowers in summer, makes a fine specimen tree.

5. There is nothing quite like the scent of freshly picked sweet peas, so typical of summer in an English country garden.

6. Love-in-a-mist (*Nigella damascena*) is almost the ideal fast-growing annual, with its combination of feathery leaves and pretty flowers, and the bonus that its seedpods are ideal for flower arranging.

Stephen Busbridge's choices:

1. The snowdrop, because it's a tough little plant and survives even the worst weather.

2. I admire the way the strap-like leaves of agapanthus show off the flowers so perfectly.

3. The silver birch (*Betula pendula*) is indispensable. It's a really good-value medium-sized tree, with attractive bark and, if you're lucky, impressive catkins.

4. The blue cedar (*Cedrus atlantica* 'Glauca') is one of the most elegant large conifers and looks as though it was designed to be grown as a specimen tree on grass.

5. I'm very fond of coleus. They are easy to grow from seed and provide a huge range of colours and leaf shapes.

6. For me, the flowering of chrysanthemums marks the onset of autumn, and their flower colours are often suitably autumnal, too.

THE MILL HOUSE, SEBERGHAM

When Kay Jefferson and her architect husband Richard bought the Mill House in the mid-1970s, they took on a formidable task. The house was old and handsome but needed much conversion work, while its 4 acres of potential garden was either rough field or a sea of concrete flooring and semi-derelict sheds. And though there were fine trees on the boundaries, there were none at all on their own land. Kay remembers that when her eldest daughter was in her pram the only shady place to put her on sunny days was in the coal shed.

However, the site's attractions outweighed its difficulties. Sebergham is a peaceful hamlet tucked into a valley bottom in the rolling agricultural landscape between Carlisle and Penrith. And the Jeffersons' land was not only sheltered by surrounding small hills but had the priceless assets of the mill stream by the house and the gentle River Caldew along one boundary.

While Richard tackled the house, Kay embarked on the garden. She says of it, 'I've tried to let the plants have their say but to have my say, too, and to make things look as though they just happened, even though in fact I keep a firm but discreet controlling hand in the background.' She works by educated instinct rather than conscious plan. Trained as a textile designer before becoming a garden designer, she thinks naturally in terms of shape and texture as well as colour. Sophisticated combinations of all three elements are characteristic of the Mill House style.

In the early years, when she had a young family and little spare time, the garden she made was relatively orthodox, with lawns and borders designed for instant colour. It was only about eighteen years ago, when she removed lawns near the house and fences further away, that the garden in its present form began to develop, not as the result of a grand plan but as a steadily expanding assemblage of separate areas. Though each area has its own atmosphere and style, all are cunningly designed to knit into a coherent whole.

The garden's 'second coming' began with the Gravel Garden, which took the place of the lawns to the south of the house. Now cistus and the quite tender pink-flowered *Phlomis italica* flourish against the house wall, while in the gravel-covered scraps of limey

Looking across the Gravel Garden to the house.

OPPOSITE It is difficult, given the lush naturalistic planting around it, to believe that the Mill House pond is not more than a decade old. In the foreground, water pours over the weir.

ABOVE A seat at the far end of the wildflower meadow makes a perfect spot for watching the bird life along the River Cardew.

soil at floor level osteospermums, iris, thymes and pinks do equally well. 'On sunny mornings,' says Kay, 'this part of the garden takes on the feel of a French gîte, and breakfast outside is one of life's heady pleasures.'

At about the same time, the Jeffersons dug out the silted-up mill stream and created a pond. 'Richard hired a mini-digger and spent several hilarious hours one drizzly February day trying to master it. It was so difficult to imagine that the ugly brown bomb crater we created would ever be a thing of beauty.' Now, though, the whole area is a sea of self-seeding primulas, iris and ligularias, from which rises a magnificent stand of *Gunnera manicata*.

Beyond the Gravel Garden lies what was once a purely functional kitchen garden but is now a more formal potager. Kay says, 'I know the paths are too narrow. I wouldn't dare do it like this if I were designing for anyone else but I wanted that childhood feeling of being engulfed by plants.'

Next you come to a 60-foot-long and deeply unaesthetic concrete shed rendered invisible by shrubs and climbers. The overwhelming sea of flower and foliage looks entirely natural and

A cobbled corner of the gravelled courtyard near the house, with its Mediterranean planting.

untamed, but despite the fact that it is on a precipitous slope and ends in a damp ditch, it actually gets a good deal of discreet attention from Kay's secateurs. Here as elsewhere she aims to 'work with nature, not fight it'. Beyond that again is a second, hidden gravelled area which has become an important part of the garden. 'We spend a lot of evenings here. It's the only part of the garden that gets the sun all day and of course gravel retains heat. As soon as you come past the hedge it hits you like a wave.'

Over the stream, instead of being a series of relatively small compartments, the garden assumes a quite different character and scale. You are confronted by an expanse of undulating lawn and beyond that a spectacular long border. The lawn was originally meadow – hence the undulations – while the border is curved like a flattened horseshoe with a freely scalloped front edge. 'We didn't want to flatten out the humps and hollows of the lawn, so I tried to make the curves of the border echo them.' The planting here

manages the difficult feat of including many special treasures within a controlled if slightly unorthodox colour scheme which from the end nearest the stream runs through lilac, purple, blue, orange, yellow and red. 'I know Jekyll would have put the blues at the ends but I just love putting blue next to orange.'

A narrow secret path has always run through the long border at the back, separating herbaceous plants from shrubs. Nowadays, behind the shrubs is a second border, held together by its use of grasses and forming a 'bridge' between the main garden and its next and newest and largest section: the wildflower meadow. This is an actual meadow, which as far as the Jeffersons know has never been ploughed and which until a few years ago was let out as sheep pasture. When the sheep were banished, a vast range of grasses, plus buttercups, oxlips, harebells, dame's violet, lady's smock and many other wild flowers quickly re-emerged. At first, the Jeffersons 'just mowed some paths through it in interesting shapes'. Since then, the right-hand side, particularly, has received the attention of Kay's discreetly controlling hand. 'I've got some serious trees here now.' These include oaks, such as *Quercus rubra* and *Q. coccinea*; beeches, including *Fagus sylvatica* 'Zlatia', *F.s.* 'Dawyck Gold' and the cut-leaved beech, *F.s.* var. *heterophylla* 'Aspleniifolia'; and many unusual rowans and acers. In twenty years' time, this side will be as much woodland glade as wildflower meadow. For the moment, though, Kay says, 'It's such a joy as it is. We walk through it often, morning and evening, and it's beautiful in spring and still beautiful in autumn.'

The garden comes to an end at the far edge of the wildflower meadow. There, an apparently natural but in fact cunningly created arbour of living willow forms a hidden retreat among the trees beside the River Caldew. It's a place from which the Jeffersons can look back over the whole 4 acres of their remarkable achievement.

The garden is open by appointment to small groups (telephone 01697 476472). Because of difficulties with parking, the garden is unable to accommodate large groups.

Cistus × purpureus 'Alan Fradd'

Dianthus 'Pike's Pink'

Primula vulgaris

Abutilon vitifolium

PLANT CHOICES

Kay Jefferson's selection of favourite plants combines colour, scent, airy graceful height and memories of childhood.

1. Purple fennel (*Foeniculum vulgare* 'Purpureum') is stunning all year. It has lovely new foliage in spring, height and texture in summer, and scent in autumn; and it looks wonderful in frost. As if that weren't enough, it's a magnificent foil for so many other plants.

2. In late summer *Verbena bonariensis* offers similar qualities: height without bulk, and movement. I love plants which move. It's particularly useful because it's in its full glory when many other things are getting to look rather tired.

3. The primrose (*Primula vulgaris*) is a memory plant for me. It takes me back to my childhood in the south-west. I also like the way it's so small that it makes you get down on your knees to appreciate it.

4. I have to choose the rose 'Paul's Himalayan Musk' for its one brief moment of absolute magnificence. I have it growing through an old apple tree, where its flowers mimic the earlier apple blossom.

5. I'm very fond of the tissue-paper flowers of cistuses. 'Alan Fradd', with white, purple-blotched flowers, is particularly beautiful. After rain there's sometimes the bonus of the fleeting 'cigar smell' of its foliage.

6. Another choice based on childhood memories is the whole range of old-fashioned pinks. I love them because their pincushions of colour in so many subtle shades add something unique to a design. And their scent! I think perfume is one of the key elements in a garden – and one that's often forgotten.

7. The grass *Stipa gigantea* offers the same sort of virtues as fennel and verbena: height together with grace and movement. It looks particularly lovely after rain or in evening light.

8. *Iris* 'Langport Wren' is only 1 foot tall, has deep purple flowers with speckles of orange on the falls, and just flowers and flowers and flowers.

9. I have *Abutilon vitifolium* in various colour forms and I love them all. It's a plant to make you go 'Wow!' It's so generous with its flowers and gives such a display that I don't mind that it only lasts around five years.

10. Plants don't have to be rare or difficult to be good. More and more I find I love plants that are easy, look after themselves and self-seed generously. *Digitalis purpurea* 'Alba' is a perfect example. And it can look positively elegant in the right place – lighting up a dark corner, say.

11. It is the deceptiveness of *Morina longifolia* that makes me love it, I think – the way it seems to be just a thistle when it's not in flower, and then a spike of fantastic flowers appears, white with a drop of purply pink hanging out of them.

12. *Helleborus foetidus* 'Wester Flisk' is at its best when all else fails, and reminds you that there is still life in the garden – that a new season is just around the corner.

CORBY CASTLE, GREAT CORBY

The garden at Corby Castle near Carlisle is remarkable because it was one of the earliest gardens in the country to make conscious dramatic use of a picturesque natural setting. Equally remarkably, given its fame in the eighteenth and early nineteenth centuries, it was largely forgotten in the later nineteenth and for much of the twentieth, partly because for many years the estate was let to tenants. Also, the garden had by then begun to show its age: trees had either died or grown too large, self-seeding sycamores and *Rhododendron ponticum* smothered more desirable plants and many of the garden's most striking architectural features had been stolen or destroyed. Rescue had become a matter of urgency, but because of the scale of the garden and the costs involved it seemed unlikely. The third remarkable fact about Corby, however, is that in the past few years a complete programme of restoration, reinvigoration and even reinvention has been undertaken by its new owners, Lord and Lady Ballyedmond.

The garden's main creators were two members of the Howard family. Thomas Howard inherited the estate in 1708 and transformed it over the next thirty-five years. Describing Corby's situation as 'grotesque and uncommon yet beautiful', he saw it as something to be treasured and turned to dramatic effect. The castle sits on top of well-wooded red sandstone bluffs above the broad reaches of the River Eden. On the river's far side are more hills and the village of Wetheral, while the Lake District fells fill the distant skyline. Thomas Howard's design skilfully made the most of all these features. Its hinge was the Green Walk, a broad flat grassed promenade some 600 metres long, which he made beside the river at the bottom of the bluffs. It was, as he said proudly, 'beautified all along with grotoes and statues of the rural daeities'. Both along the Green Walk and on subsidiary paths winding up the bluffs he installed carved inscriptions to act as stage directions telling visitors what to feel. These may well have been the earliest such inscriptions in an English garden; certainly they predated the famous ones by the poet William Shenstone at his Midlands garden, the Leasowes, which were installed in the 1740s.

LEFT The Great Cascade, from the Temple of Venus at the top to the basin (with the statue of Nelson) at the bottom.

RIGHT, ABOVE Looking from the terrace down the broad expanses of the River Eden. The river is in two sections here, divided by an artificial island. The island was constructed by the monks of Wetheral Priory as a way to guide salmon into salmon coops, which still exist. The island was planted with trees by Thomas Howard. On a map of 1729 they show as tiny saplings; many are now so tall that they arch right across to the trees on the bank above the Green Walk.

RIGHT, BELOW The monsters at the top of the Cascade.

At the southern end of the Green Walk, furthest from the house, the vista ends in a classical temple, the Tempietta, positioned on a small mound and reached by a small flight of stone steps. It retains its original painted decorations on either side of its doorway and – for vandalism is nothing new – its eighteenth-century graffiti. In contrast to this charming miniature toy, the end of the Green Walk nearest the house is dignified by one of the most grandly astonishing sights in any British garden: a spring-fed Cascade which tumbles 40 metres down a series of steps and small pools cut into the cliff. At the top it falls from the grotesque jaws of stone monsters which leer from the base of another temple, the Temple of Venus, and it descends to a large circular stone basin, from which it is fed into the river. In the nineteenth century, in a bizarre outburst of patriotism, a statue of Nelson was added to the middle of the basin. Howard also had a semicircular stone bastion built out into the river, from which a flight of steps, surmounted by an arch known as the Water Gate, leads down to the water. Stands were built here from which spectators could watch plays performed high above on 'the platform of the Cascade'. One of these plays was Thomas Howard's own adaptation of Milton's *Comus*, at the close of which, when Ithuriel waves his wand, 'the sluices are opened, and a large mass of water rolls down into the basin below'. That must have been quite a sight.

Thomas's son Philip made only minor changes, such as extending the walks beyond the Tempietta and allowing almost unlimited access to the garden. Sadly, that last change led to the vandalism at the Tempietta and the theft and destruction of statues

and inscriptions by visitors who, as one contemporary said, 'left neither a seat, nor the smooth bark of a tree unmutilated with names and low verses'. It was Philip's son Henry Howard who made the second major contribution to the garden. Soldier, traveller, antiquary, architect, gardener and collector, this man of many talents and interests managed the difficult feat of respecting his grandfather's achievements while adding to them in his own style. He had the Temple of Venus and the Cascade restored, a dovecote in the park turned into an additional temple and an elaborate stone well head named after his wife Catherine built among the woods on the bluffs above the Green Walk. Near the castle (which was remodelled between 1812 and 1817 in Classical style in red sandstone quarried on the estate) he created an unusually elaborate frontage to the fine walled garden.

It was essentially a rather tired but unaltered version of this landscape which the Ballyedmonds acquired in 1993. Since then the Tempietta, the 'dovecote temple', the Cascade and the flights of steps on either side of it have all been completely repaired and restored. Overgrown and overhanging trees have been cut back to make the drama of the Cascade fully visible. Similar thinning has been carried out throughout the woodland, where there has also been much replanting, particularly of large-leaved rhododendrons such as *R. falconeri*. Paths have been reinstated and resurfaced, and everywhere urns and statues have been introduced to take the place of those lost over the years, with the result that the Green Walk, in particular, now has much of its original impact.

In the early nineteenth century Henry and Catherine Howard had wanted to make a grand terrace on the river side of the castle. In those days, though, the technology didn't exist to enable it to be anchored safely into the steeply sloping and spring-riddled bank below. Nowadays it does; and so, therefore, does the terrace, a red sandstone creation of considerable grandeur, held by piles dug and

cemented deep into the rock below. 'In effect,' says Lord Ballyedmond, 'I have carried out their intentions.' The shape and planting of the terrace beds was decided by discussions between Lady Ballyedmond and the garden designer and historian Elizabeth Banks, while the choice of plants for the still ferociously steep bank below the terrace has been entirely Lady Ballyedmond's.

The garden is open to the public only very occasionally to small specialist groups. However, the theatrical climax of the Cascade, the Green Walk and the Tempietta is clearly visible from the public footpath along the far side of the river, reached from Wetheral village.

OPPOSITE The east front of the house of 1812–17. The unusual single-storey arcaded sections flanking the portico are conservatories, designed to be used by Catherine Howard, who was a devoted gardener.

ABOVE The mighty stone fountain which now acts as a centrepiece in the walled garden.

FOLLOWING PAGE The steps up from the Cascade, and the grottoes beneath.

Azara microphylla

Callicarpa bodinieri var. *giraldii* 'Profusion'

Winter aconite (*Eranthis hyemalis*)

PLANT CHOICES

Lady Ballyedmond suggests some of her favourite plants.

1. Witch hazels do well at Corby high on the river bank in partial shade and relatively neutral soil. The scented *Hamamelis mollis* is one of the finest winter-flowering shrubs and works well either as a specimen or in groups.

2. The winter aconite (*Eranthis hyemalis*) provides a nice sunny yellow under trees in early spring, and juxtaposed with the blue of *Iris reticulata* makes a gay, but not garish, display.

3. The soft blue, spring-flowering clematis 'Frances Rivis' grows well against the south-facing wall of the castle and occasionally provides a second flush of bloom in summer.

4. *Erythronium* 'Pagoda', a vigorous variety of dog's-tooth violet growing to 20 centimetres tall and with sulphur-yellow flowers, is good for naturalizing. It does well at Corby in a well-drained transitional area between shrub bed and woodland.

5. Don't underestimate ivy. If you have space to let it cover large areas, it can look splendid. At Corby, the ivy that cascades down, and overhangs, the rock face below the west terrace of the castle is still going strong nearly two hundred years after it was mentioned by Catherine Howard. It was known then, and is still known, as the Chancellor's Wig.

6. Boston ivy (*Parthenocissus tricuspidata*) turns wonderful shades of red and purple from August onwards on the south and east walls of the castle and perfectly complements the deep pink of our Lazonby sandstone. We are propagating more to spread it around the renovated estate buildings.

7. *Potentilla* 'Gibson's Scarlet', a bright red potentilla with a charming delicacy of form, is good value in the summer border.

8. The flowers of *Rosa × odorata* 'Mutabilis' begin bright orange and pass through yellow and pink to a reddish copper. It has a delicate airy elegance that few plants possess, and is seen at its best when its neighbours are in the green and not flowering. Our single plant grows in a sheltered position, on a concave bank which we call the Bowl, and is one of the most beautiful plants in the garden.

9. Among the many varieties of rose in the new rose garden, 'Mister Lincoln' is truly outstanding for the depth of colour of its red flowers and for its scent. It appears to be easy to please as to conditions.

10. The flowers of *Azara microphylla*, an elegant evergreen shrub from Chile, provide a wonderful vanilla scent in spring. It thrives at Corby in the shelter of an east-facing wall.

11. The tree peony *Paeonia delavayi*, with single flowers the colour of the finest Burmese rubies, blooms high on the west terrace bank in summer. It is a show-stopper. Its flowering season seems to lengthen as it grows older. It resents cold winter winds and looked rather sickly for a spell in late February. It is not pretty when it loses its leaves, so it is best planted amongst other shrubs.

12. The bright lilac berries of *Callicarpa bodinieri* 'Profusion' create a wonderful autumn contrast with the faded red brick-work of the 'Smoke Wall' against which this shrub is grown here.

GARTH HOUSE, BRAMPTON

When David Tate and his wife Sandra bought Garth House on the edge of the small market town of Brampton in the far north of Cumbria in the mid-1990s, the garden in which the dignified, late-Georgian red sandstone house was set was a simple 4 acres of shelter belts, shrubberies and lawns. It did not, David decided, make an effective setting for the house. 'There was a lack of major architectural interest and of any real flower borders.' Thinking about how to change it, he fell suddenly and passionately in love with gardening – so much so that 'retirement' means that instead of working twelve or fourteen hours a day in his business he now spends the same amount of time in his garden. As a result, and because 'I love drama and contrasts', Garth House now has not one garden but a whole Catherine wheel of them, surrounding the house in a dazzling array of different styles.

These gardens include a sunken formal garden, a wild garden, a woodland walk leading to a wildlife pond, a Japanese garden, a parterre-cum-potager, an Italian garden, a pool garden, a Mediterranean garden and even a Zen garden. 'They are not really "garden rooms",' David says. 'Though I sympathize with that approach, I wanted something more flowing and relaxed.' Of course, as he adds with a wry smile, garden creation on this scale and at this speed 'isn't a cheap option'. In this case it involved employing up to nine men for four years, shifting hundreds of tons of topsoil, importing similar amounts of stone, building walls, terraces, bridges, pavilions, fountains, rockeries and streams, and planting over five thousand new plants. He admits to having had moments when he felt, as he puts it, 'financially bruised'. But he is not just the overall controller and cheque writer. While he is happy to call in experts for advice (which he sometimes takes, sometimes doesn't, and almost always modifies), much of the design, the landscaping, and the choice and positioning of the plants is his.

Among the garden's many sections three in particular stand out. The creation of the striking octagonal sunken formal garden adjoining the house involved shifting 175 tons of soil to make its central amphitheatre-like lawn and using the stone from three barns to build sheltering walls and a flagged terrace between it and the house.

The tranquil central section of the stream in the Japanese Garden, with a Japanese-style bridge and a range of acers, bamboos and conifers (some clipped in Oriental 'cloud' style).

Already those walls are swathed in roses and clematis, while deep and richly planted herbaceous borders run around the perimeter. These include many peonies, which also feature elsewhere throughout the garden, because David loves their unashamedly theatrical beauty. A fine stone fountain acts as a central focus and an elaborate stone pavilion as a partial vista-stopper at the garden's furthest point. The pavilion deliberately allows a glimpse of the considerable wild garden beyond, which carries on tantalizingly out of sight around a corner.

David's fascination with Japan – he lived and did business for some years in the Far East – inspired what is perhaps the garden's most remarkable section. Three and a half years ago, Garth House had a flat tennis court. Now in its place it has a bravura recreation of a mountainous Japanese landscape. 'I love the way early Japanese gardens created the effect of a "landscape in miniature". That's what I've tried to achieve here.' He positioned 200 tons of red sandstone to act as 'mountains' and created between them a sunken stream that cascades down to a series of pools. The dense but discriminating surrounding planting includes bamboos (over thirty different kinds), acers (nearly fifty different kinds), ferns (over eighty different kinds), many rhododendrons and azaleas, and conifers 'controlled' as semi-bonsai. The upper end of the garden is marked by an imposing Japanese-style boundary wall, topped by imported Japanese blue-glazed tiles attached to a custom-made wooden framework – all made and put in place by David and his full-time 'construction man'.

The Exotic Garden near by is in fact three sections in one. First comes what David calls the Italian Garden, its formal design and

many statues almost swallowed by the dramatic foliage of cordylines and palms. The palms are numerous *Trachycarpus fortunei* in the ground and a sizeable specimen of *Butia capitata* in a pot – which, remarkably in an inland garden in north Cumbria, stays out over winter. This area also features equally exotic giant summer bedding, including a profusion of cannas and bananas. The shadier side, towards the house, modulates into a fern-rich courtyard, dominated by two huge *Dicksonia antarctica*, which survive outside in the ground unprotected. Beyond is what is as much a giant conservatory as a covered and heated swimming pool, since its humid heat allows David to grow here rainforest plants that it would be impossible to grow outside. At one end he has created a special bed in which large specimens of these exotic foliage plants create a jungle-like atmosphere, while others in pots are scattered

The Italian Garden adjoining the swimming pool, with its border which bizarrely but effectively combines cottage garden favourites (such as foxgloves) and, later in the season, tender exotics used as bedding. Notable plants here include *Alstroemeria* 'Princess Beatrix' in the foreground, the lush leaves of Chinese gooseberry (*Actinidia chinensis* 'Deliciosa') threatening to envelop the central statue of David, the evergreen *Clematis armandii* on the wall in the distance and the white-flowered *Paeonia lactiflora* 'Solange' in front of the third statue.

In the Mediterranean Garden, gravel up to 15 centimetres thick, and the shelter of surrounding walls and trellising, allows the palm on the left, *Phoenix canariensis*, to survive in the ground year round, though it does get some winter protection. The tree in the pot in the foreground is an olive (*Olea europaea*). To the left and right there are specimens of *Yucca gloriosa* and in the Cretan pot in the background is a fine *Agave ferox*.

along the pool's remaining three sides. Finally, beyond the pool, is the Mediterranean Garden. Here, the original soil has had quantities of gravel added to it, plus a top dressing of 8 inches of gravel, because David is adamant that for the successful cultivation of tender exotics in the inland north 'drainage is much more important than temperature'. As a result, agaves and even a 10-foot-high *Phoenix canariensis* flourish happily here. He confesses, though, that the latter, a palm tree, benefits from a giant 'cloche' in winter.

David has brought to his garden, as he did his business, inventiveness, energy and a clear-sighted ability to carry his plans through to completion. As a result he has created within a remarkably short time an impressive and individual garden.

The garden is open by appointment (telephone 01697 72952 or email deejate@lineone.net).

Acer palmatum 'Ôsakazuki'

Acer palmatum 'Shindeshôjô'

Phyllostachys vivax f. *aureocaulis*

PLANT CHOICES

David Tate chooses a few favourite plants.

1. What I call 'primordial plants' are my first love. These include tree ferns, which have been around since the age of the dinosaurs. The easiest and probably the hardiest species, *Dicksonia antarctica*, loves the moist cool climate of Cumbria, which is so like that of the west coast of New Zealand, where it grows in profusion.

2. The acers are the stars of our Japanese Garden. *A. palmatum* 'Shindeshôjô' has the most gorgeous iridescent pink foliage in the spring, while the luminous vermilion display of *A.p.* 'Ôsakazuki' lasts for weeks during autumn. If you're pushed for space, *A.p.* 'Red Pygmy' is a good choice. It looks fantastic all year round, with the bonus that it turns butter yellow in the autumn.

3. Bamboos are a boon for any gardener who wants to create exotic effects. They seem to take you into another world. Two of my favourites are *Phyllostachys vivax* f. *aureocaulis*, which grows over 4 metres tall and is magnificent both in colour and form, and *Fargesia robusta*, a well-behaved medium-sized bamboo that will grow just about anywhere.

4. We have quite a few varieties of peonies in the borders, particularly in the Sunken Garden. They can sometimes be tricky but 'Sarah Bernhardt' and 'Bowl of Beauty' are both reliable.

5. My wife, Sandra, has planted about twenty magnolias in the past ten years and her favourite is *Magnolia grandiflora*. In its sheltered position on the south-west side of the house, it rewards us with huge cream flowers, some as much as 20 centimetres across, at the end of summer each year.

Cairnbeck,
near Irthington

When ten years ago John Main and his wife Marisa approached retirement after their respective distinguished careers in horticulture – which he ended as Director of Horticulture at the Royal Botanic Garden in Edinburgh, she in the herbarium there – they worked out what they needed. Their retirement home had to be new or somewhere that did not need any work done to it. And it had to have a big garden, with a stream. However, having looked at and rejected houses from Perthshire to Yorkshire, they finally bought Cairnbeck in John's native hamlet of Newtown, near Irthington in the countryside north of Carlisle, which didn't meet a single one of those specifications. The single-storey cottage is a conversion of the old stone outbuildings of the adjacent farmhouse, there is no stream and the area for a garden was tiny: 100 feet by 60 feet.

When they arrived, there wasn't even a real garden. 'A few undistinguished shrubs, a lot of grass, a lot of stone from demolished outbuildings and a lot of rubbish' is John's crisp summary. Their garden is now a model of how much you can squeeze into a tiny plot while still producing an aesthetically pleasing effect.

Coming down only at weekends for several years, they were seduced into bringing with them examples of all their favourite plants from their Edinburgh garden – 'We simply tried to grow too much,' says Marisa – and after a few years there had to be a drastic thinning-out. Otherwise, though, their professional skills enabled them to get the vast majority of things right. As a result, their garden is now a model of how you can squeeze so much into a tiny plot yet still create something which is visually attractive.

The Mains began by using the stone already on site to make several walls across the garden. This was done partly to get rid of the stone, partly to provide homes for some of John's beloved alpines and partly to help make the garden seem bigger by emphasizing its width and dividing it into areas. Then the hollow alpine stone walls needed a filling of soil. Where was it to come from? The garden. What to do with the hole left after the soil had been removed?

The hybrids of *Rhododendron yakushimanum* are some of the most spectacular shrubs for late spring and early summer. The one in the foreground here is 'Bashful' and the blue poppy growing alongside is *Meconopsis* 'Lingholm'. The slender white trunk in the background which, with the pergola and the dovecote, helps to add vertical interest is *Betula utilis* var. *jacquemontii* 'Inverleith'.

Turn it into a pond, of course, since they hadn't got that stream they wanted. John says firmly, 'To my mind a garden has to have water. Anyway, it's good for the wildlife.' Though space also had to be found for John's bantams and canaries, the overriding intention was to create suitable homes for such a wide range of plants that the garden would provide year-round interest. Hence the dense planting in a maze of specialist beds, each designed to provide a specific habitat for a specific type of plant, as well as many other containers of one sort or another, both for plants and for creatures.

When the Mains arrived, there were no trees or big shrubs in the garden at all. As a result, the site was completely open to winds from the south and, worse, the east. Now the astonishing roll call of trees and shrubs includes 12 magnolias, 9 eucryphias, 4 sorbus, 2 betulas, 2 hamamelis, 2 acers, a metasequoia and the unusual autumn-colouring *Nyssa sylvatica* 'Wisley Bonfire'. These provide shelter and shade for John's other great love, woodland plants, such as trilliums, arisaemas, tricyrtis and dactylorhizas. Growing so many trees in such a small space is possible only because of Marisa's devoted and skilful pruning. The principle behind it is to 'layer' the planting, maximizing the use of the ground by steadily raising the canopy of trees and shrubs so that large herbaceous plants occupy the next level down and bulbs and small herbaceous plants the lowest one. The same space-maximizing methods are applied to the garden's immaculate greenhouses, cold frames, troughs and animal pens. No inch is wasted and often two or three structures of different sizes and functions occupy the same area.

John confesses that, after a professional life spent making plant collections, he can't resist continuing to make them in retirement. In and out of the ground, Cairnbeck has collections of, for example, daphnes, corydalis, hepaticas, double hellebores, celmisias and roscoeas. Some of the last two far-from-easy groups are enjoying life at Cairnbeck so much that they are self-seeding into the walls and gravel paths. It is not just John who makes collections: Marisa has her own, of ferns and snowdrops. And such is the Mains' skill that many of the plants in the garden are unusual, difficult or tender – and sometimes all three at once. A good example is the Chilean climber *Latua pubiflora*, commercially unavailable in this country yet flourishing on the house wall at Cairnbeck behind a fine 7-foot specimen of *Daphne bholua*.

OPPOSITE It is sometimes difficult to remember that this small garden, with its complicated design and dense planting from all over the world, is in fact carved out of the edge of a perfectly ordinary Cumbrian field. In the distance to the south-east is the outline of Carrick fell.

ABOVE The magnolia 'Jane' is in flower at the back of this terrace, while in the paving are a pink *Phlox subulata* hybrid and the yellow flowers of *Narcissus* 'Sun Disc'. On the left are double aquilegias.

A section of a raised bed, with the bold sword-shaped silvery foliage of *Celmisia coriacea* var. *semicordata* in the foreground and phlox hybrids beyond providing masses of colour.

John grows many of the unusual plants here from seed — often seed that he has collected himself in the wild. Equally often, such plants have been gifts from friends, either in this country or abroad. Notwithstanding personal origins and associations, though, when despite Marisa's devoted pruning plants finally outgrow their space, they are ruthlessly removed. John explains firmly that regret is not an option because 'There are too many other beautiful plants to try. And, anyway, you can always re-propagate and start all over again.' His wife sums up the gardening philosophy behind the garden when she adds, 'Nothing here is set in tablets of stone. The way the garden keeps changing is a real part of the pleasure we get from it.'

The garden opens by appointment (telephone 01697 742474) and John Main lectures on horticulture to gardening groups and societies.

Acer griseum

Hamamelis mollis

Celmisia coriacea var. *semicordata*

PLANT CHOICES

John Main chooses twelve plants, all of which are ideal for a small garden.

1. The paperbark maple (*Acer griseum*) is an excellent tree for a small garden, providing interest throughout the year, especially in the autumn with its rich red tints and throughout the winter with its peeling cinnamon bark.
2. *Eucryphia* × *nymansensis* 'Nymansay' is a large shrub or small tree which provides flowers in August and September when very few other woody plants do.
3. *Hamamelis mollis* 'Pallida' is excellent for January colour and scent and can even be forced indoors for Christmas flowers. Rich yellow autumn colour is a bonus.
4. I like all lilies, so it is very difficult to single out one species or hybrid. Plant as many as you can, and with careful selection you can have them in flower from late spring well into the autumn.
5. Once the petals of *Magnolia salicifolia* 'Wada's Memory' reflex they remind me of a cloud of white butterflies. This is not a difficult plant to grow.
6. Candelabra primulas are indispensable for their stature, range of colours, long flowering period and ability to freely hybridize.
7. *Camellia* × *williamsii* 'Donation' is the best camellia for the north of England. It is very reliable and always produces a good show of colour in early spring.
8. *Daphne mezereum* is easy to grow and reliably produces its scented flowers early in the year.
9. *Roscoea cautleyoides* is a hardy ginger that gives the garden an almost tropical feel.
10. *Celmisia coriacea* var. *semicordata* has attractive silver leaves with large white daisy flowers. It grows so well in this part of the country that it self-seeds.
11. Himalayan blue poppies provide the garden with an air of grace. *Meconopsis* 'Lingholm' is reputedly of Cumbrian origin. It is a reliable perennial and not difficult to grow from seed.
12. I recommend *Lewisia cotyledon* hybrids for the sheer range of their vibrant colours.

OTHER GARDENS

Buckbarrow House

BUCKBARROW HOUSE, GOSFORTH

John Maddison has cunningly designed a series of tiny gardens-within-a-garden, densely planted in a range of styles, from cottage garden to Oriental, around a modern estate house on the edge of Gosforth village. The back garden has the disadvantage of a public footpath running through it, but he has skilfully turned it into an advantage by using it to 'borrow' views up and down through neighbouring gardens. In the same way a false gate at the end of the garden 'borrows' the view across fields to the nearest fell. This is a garden full of inspiring ideas for anyone keen on plants but wrestling with limited space and a difficult site.

The garden opens under the National Gardens Scheme.

CARDEW LODGE, DALSTON

Cardew Lodge, outside the village of Dalston, is a long, low, castellated, red sandstone house, built as a hunting lodge for a General Lowther in the nineteenth century. The main feature of its grounds is a splendid walled garden, with elaborate 'Gothick' windows and buttresses and a built-in circular gardener's cottage. Owner David Mallison has transformed the original traditional kitchen-and-cutting garden, with its simple rectangular layout, into an ambitious ornamental garden to a very individual swirling design. His wife Margery explains, 'We like a naturally flowing garden, not one that's too stiff.' Its focal point, apart from two huge herbaceous borders against the walls on either side, is an elaborate water garden. Around it is dense planting in which cottage garden foxgloves mingle amicably with exotic yuccas. Recently, part of the adjacent field has been turned into an even bigger water and bog garden, consisting of four substantial ponds. Here the planting is based on natives, such as bulrushes and flag irises (*Iris pseudacorus*), so that the garden merges gently and stylishly into the surrounding landscape.

The garden is open each summer over a weekend for a local charity.

Cardew Lodge

Gatesgarth

GATESGARTH, WATERMILLOCK

Sadie Quick's 6-acre garden high above Ullswater offers dramatic views of the lake and of the fells on its far side. Over the past twenty years, she has turned this steeply sloping and all-too-well-watered site into what is essentially an informal woodland garden, with slightly more open and formal areas closer to the house. It is predominantly a garden for spring, when rhododendrons and azaleas are the main flowering shrubs, while drifts of hundreds of self-seeding daffodils, Himalayan primulas, meconopsis and *Lysichiton americanum* colonize every damp patch and run along the edges of the garden's many miniature streams.

The garden opens most years in May or June for a changing cast of Sadie's favourite local charities. The openings are advertised in local newspapers.

Glen Artney

Graythwaite Hall

GLEN ARTNEY, ARMATHWAITE

Glen Artney is everyone's idea of a laid-back but stylish country garden. David and Jean Tomlinson have owned their walled 1 acre (once the kitchen garden of Armathwaite Castle) for almost forty years. The garden has changed during that time according to the changing demands of family life (first three young sons, now a gaggle of grandchildren) but has always been a proper country garden. Jean describes it as 'an extension of the house, a place for children, a place to eat, a place to grow our favourite vegetables, while also of course a place we try to make attractive. But it's meant to be relaxed and relaxing. It isn't for show.' Another necessary ingredient of a country garden is of course animals, and apart from the family dog Glen Artney has wild birds, frogs in the pond, hedgehogs under the summerhouse and doves in the barn; there are even slow worms, rescued and brought into the garden by the Tomlinson boys years ago. While vegetable gardener David loves neatness, regularity and straight lines, ornamental gardener Jean likes her borders to have bold curves and the plants to be, in her phrase, 'more rampant': 'I don't like bittiness. I like to use plants in drifts, so that a whole border knits together.' Despite its deliberate unshowiness, there is a surprising visual richness here, which derives precisely from those stimulating contrasts between neatness and looseness, straightness and curviness.

The garden opens under the National Gardens Scheme.

GRAYTHWAITE HALL, NEAR ULVERSTON

At the end of the nineteenth century, Colonel Thomas Sandys gave the subsequently famous garden designer Thomas Mawson his first major commission, to redesign the garden of Graythwaite Hall so that it would provide a suitable setting for his imposing new version of the house. Today, much of this historically important garden is still as Mawson designed it. It also contains his plan's fine sundials, balustrading and wrought-iron work, some of it designed by his frequent collaborator, the architect Dan Gibson. Mawson's ability to fit a house and its garden into their surroundings, even right at the beginning of his career, is very apparent. Skilfully arranged terraces lead the eye out to the informal woodland beyond, while more formal areas add dignity to the house. These include an atmospheric Dutch Garden and what was once a substantial formal Rose Garden, now filled with labour-saving bergenias. This is very much a spring garden, particularly since owner Myles Sandys' father was a rhododendron enthusiast who planted many good examples along the beck that divides the more formal areas from the informal woodland beyond. It is not a showy garden but very peaceful and intensely atmospheric – and, being slightly off the beaten track, relatively unfrequented.

The garden is open from 10.00 a.m. to 6.00 p.m. daily from April until the end of August. Guided tours for groups are possible 'after hours' by arrangement. For more information, telephone 01539 531248 or visit www.graythwaitehall.co.uk.

LAKE HOUSE, CAPERNWRAY

Tony and Edwina Rickards-Collinson's garden at Lake House is really two gardens in one. Around the house is a substantial formal garden designed by Arabella Lennox-Boyd, approached along a fine avenue of standard limes (*Tilia × europaea*) and dominated by a profusion of roses with flowers in shades of deep red, pink and purple – Edwina's favourite colours. On the far side of the house, a broad stone terrace offers fine views of the garden's hidden surprise: a sizeable lake filling the shallow valley beyond. The lake is in fact artificial but its serpentine shape looks remarkably natural – which is underlined by the skilful semi-wild planting that edges both it and the path around it.

The garden opens under the National Gardens Scheme.

Lake House

MORLAND HOUSE, MORLAND

Markhams have lived at Morland House in the Eden Valley for nearly two centuries and the 4 acres of its garden contain fascinating evidence of gardening taste through many generations. There are peaceful Victorian lawns and mighty yew walks; fine herbaceous borders and a handsome beck criss-crossed by bridges in several different styles; eye-catching recent stone-built follies; and the hidden surprise of the newly restored sunken Victorian Quarry Garden, with central water features, dense surrounding planting and, at its far end, the further surprise of a long raised bed planted in a dazzling range of 'hot' flower and foliage colours.

The garden is open from 10.00 a.m. to 5.00 p.m. Monday to Saturday throughout the year to visitors to the shop (in what was once Morland House's stable block), which stocks the wares of the Markhams' Travelling Light clothing company.

QUARRY HILL HOUSE, MEALSGATE

Sitting high on a hill, with fine views inland to the Caldbeck fells and in the other direction to the Solway Firth and the hills of Dumfriesshire, this is a traditional country garden around a traditional country house. But under the ownership of Charles and Margaret Woodhouse it is also undergoing some exciting and extensive new developments. Around the house are about 3 acres of gardens, divided between relaxed mixed borders and a finely maintained traditional kitchen garden. Beyond are 25 acres of parkland and woodland, including a completely new wood, created in 2002 and consisting of 2002 trees. Most are native hardwoods but there is also a substantial sprinkling of ornamental specimens. The wood is being treated as a wildflower meadow, in keeping with the garden's determinedly wildlife-friendly policy. Meandering paths mown through it eventually lead into a recently restored area of older woodland and a chain of restored flight ponds for duck.

The garden opens under the National Gardens Scheme, occasionally for charities and for groups by appointment (telephone 01697 371225).

Morland House

Quarry Hill House

Rose Castle

Roundhill

ROSE CASTLE, DALSTON

Rose Castle, the home of the bishops of Carlisle, is an ancient building which has developed piecemeal over many centuries, as has its garden. There is an atmospheric woodland garden in what was once the moat and an orchard devoted to local varieties such as 'Carlisle Codlin' and 'Egremont Russet' where in Edwardian times there was a formal Dutch garden. Along the terraces designed in the mid-nineteenth century by Joseph Paxton, gardener Janet Queen has created colourful mainly herbaceous borders. There is also a charming 'informally formal' vegetable garden in potager style, where ornamental plants for cutting mingle effectively and decoratively with the vegetables. While this lays no claim to be a show garden, it is one of great charm and historical interest, in a particularly beautiful parkland setting, even by Cumbria's high standards.

Group visits can be arranged by appointment (email bishop.carlisle@carlislediocese.org.uk or telephone 01697 476274).

ROUNDHILL, EASEDALE

Roundhill is as much a story and a situation as a garden. Perched high on the side of a rocky fell, it offers remarkable views down Easedale. In the 1920s, its steep slope suggested to Harry Schill, a Manchester industrialist who was a founder member of the Alpine Garden Society, that its 2 acres were a natural site for a rock garden. Schill was then elderly, had lost his only son in the First World War and his wife soon after, and came to the Lakes looking for some sort of peace. He never owned the site but he stayed in the house as a paying guest, making the garden, its winding paths, raised stone-walled beds and carefully contrived 'planting pockets' with the help of the owner, who was the grandfather of the late wife of the current owner, Stuart McGlasson. By the 1930s Roundhill was famous for its extensive collection of rarities but after Schill's death it became increasingly abandoned and many of the rarities were lost. Stuart has reclaimed and extended the garden, not with the same sort of 'difficult specials' but with miniature 'good doers' which will look after themselves and self-seed sensibly. The result is a peaceful and relaxed garden with a dramatic prospect, tucked in a frequently overlooked corner at the heart of the Lake District.

The garden is open throughout the season, with an honesty box on the gate. Guided tours can be arranged by appointment (telephone 01539 435233). Parking is very limited so it is best to walk up from Grasmere village.

WOOD GHYLL, CROSTHWAITE

The garden at Wood Ghyll in the lovely Lyth Valley in the south of Cumbria is based on a dramatic combination of woodland and water. The house sits on a plateau above a miniature rocky outcrop. Below it, the garden runs down the slope to the River Lyth and then across into the woodland on the other side. Owner John Cook's great passion is rhododendrons and he grows over 100 species, planted mostly in the wild garden in the woodland across the river, where paths mown through the grass weave between the trees, and a dense planting of herbaceous moisture-lovers fills the boggiest sections by the river. Although everywhere there are John's species rhododendrons, there are also several unusual tree-sized hydrangeas as well as many eucryphias. On the other side of the river, the rocky well-drained outcrop below the house provides a suitable home for young specimens of distinctly tender rhododendron species, such as *R. edgeworthii* and *R. polyandrum*.

The garden opens as part of Crosthwaite's occasional Garden Open days, which include several other high-quality gardens.

Wood Ghyll

WOOD HALL, COCKERMOUTH

The house and garden at Wood Hall were designed by Thomas Mawson on a striking but dauntingly steep hillside outside Cockermouth. By the time Jack and Dorothy Jackson acquired it, the house had been demolished (the Jacksons live in the converted stables) and the grandiose 4-acre terraced garden, designed for the sake of the fine views along the River Isel and across to the Lorton Valley, had lost most of its original planting and much of its hard landscaping. Over the decades since, Dorothy has done a great deal to reclaim the garden by rebuilding steps and terrace walls and replanting the terrace beds. Where reclamation was impossible, she has made a new garden in a style sympathetic to the original. She has even made a garden over the foundations of the original mansion. The planting makes much use of vigorous ground-cover plants, which is sensible in a large garden that is essentially owner-maintained, but also includes a discriminating selection of high-quality trees and shrubs.

The garden is open by appointment for groups or individuals (telephone 01900 823585 or email wood-hall@ukonline.co.uk).

Wood Hall

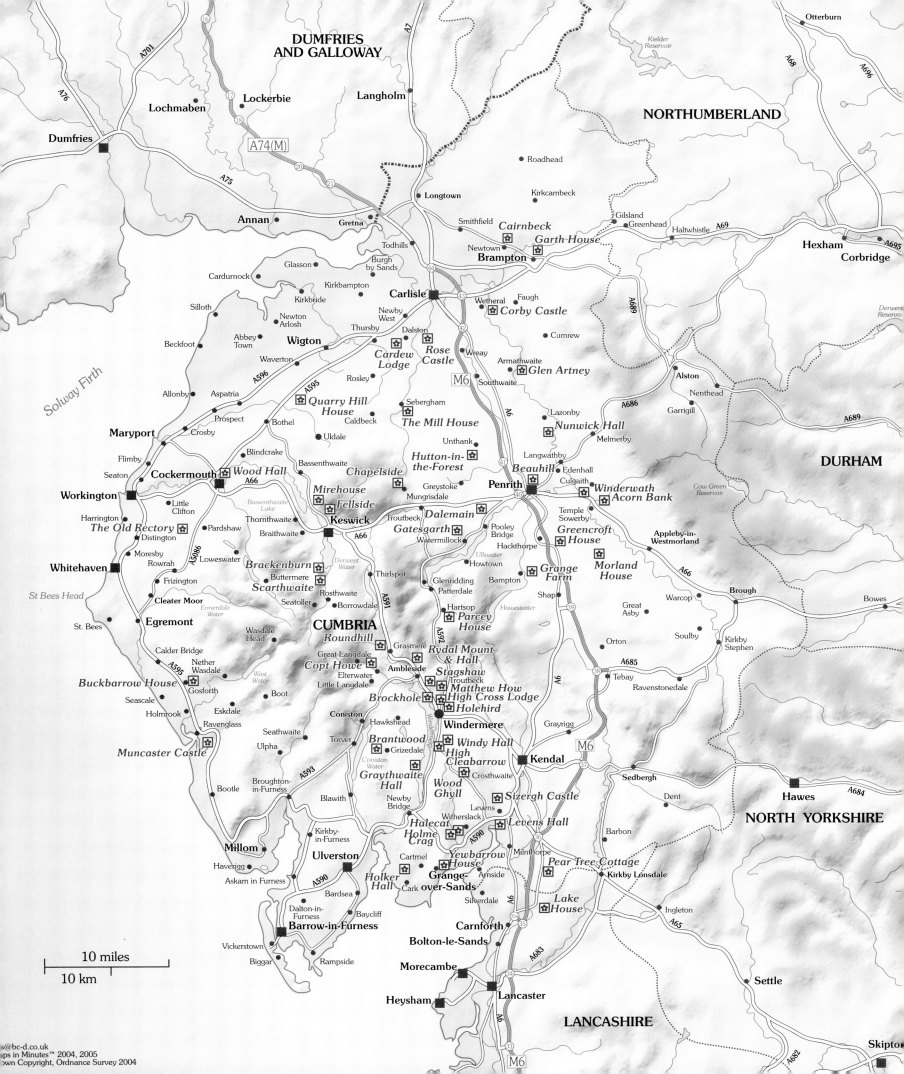

INDEX

Page references in **bold** type refer to the main entry for each garden and include illustrations within the page range. *Italic* type is used to refer to the captions for all other page references for illustrations.

A

Abelia schumannii 174
Abies
  Cephalonica 165
  concolor Lowiana Group 217
Abutilon
  vitifolium 229, *229*
  × *suntense* 117
Acanthus spinosissimus 54
Acca sellowiana 23
Acer 62, 112, *119*, 211, 228, *237*, 238, 244
  aconitifolium 124
  campestre (field maple) 145
  davidii 139
  dissectum 113
    'Atropurpureum' 83
  griseum 117, 124, 163, 190, 247, *247*
  japonicum
    'Aconitifolium' 84
    'Aureum' 117
    'Vitifolium' 117
  palmatum 123
    'Atropurpureum' *137*
    f. *atropurpurem 123*
    'Beni-hime' 124
    var. *dissectum* 113, 123, 153
      Dissectum Atropurpureum Group 22, 83
    'Higasayama' 124
    'Ōsakazuki' 241, *241*
    'Red Pygmy' 124, 241
    'Sango-kaku' ('Senkaki') 79, *79*, 93, 175
    'Shindeshōjō' 241, *241*
    'Shishigashira' 124
  shirasawanum 'Aureum' 124, *125*
Aciphylla 208
Acland, Cuthbert (Cubby) 106
Acland, Robin 201, 202
Acland, Tricia 201, 205
aconites 142, 160, 192, 235, *235*
Aconitum 216
  napellus 171
Acorn Bank **194–9**
Actaea
  simplex
    Atropurpurea Group 171
    'Brunette' 217
Actinidia chinensis 'Deliciosa' 239
Adiantum
  aleuticum 151, *151*
  pedatum 151
  venustum 151
Aegeratum leillanii 47
Aegopodium podagraria 136
Aesculus indica × *neglecta* 'Erythroblastos' 125
Agapanthus 223
  africanus 171
Agave 18, 87, 89
  ferox 240, *240*
Alchemilla 213
Allison, John 177
Allium 28, 89, 104, 123, 201
  aflatunense 161
  schoenoprasum 187
Alocasia macrorrhiza 19
Alstroemeria 'Princess Beatrix' 239
Amelanchier lamarckii 31, *31*
Anemone
  × *hupehensis* 'Hadspen Abundance' 117
  obtusiloba 175, *175*
  rivularis 175
  trullifolia 125
    'Alba' 205, *205*
Antirrhinum majus 'Liberty Classic Yellow' *47*, 51
Apiaceae 199
Aponogeton distachyos 34
apple see *Malus*
Aquilegia 117, *245*
  vulgaris 149
    'William Guinness' 28
Aralia elata 'Variegata' 99
Argyranthemum foeniculare 51
Arisaema 244
  ciliatum 188
  tortuosum var. *helleboriflolium 193*

Aronia 137
  melanocarpa 139
Aruncus 80
  dioicus 77, 216
asparagus 51
  'Franklin' 145, *145*
Asphodeline lutea 201
Asplenium scolopendrium 'Crispum Speciosum Moly' 151
Astelia 208
  nervosa 'Red Gem' *209*
Aster 104
Astilbe 28, *32*, 80, 155
Astrantia
  major
    'Claret' 26
    'Roma' 31
  maxima 199
    'Norah Barlow' *161*
Athyrium
  niponicum var. *pictum* 151
  pedatum 'Japonicum' 89
Attwood, Tom 132
azaleas see *Rhododendron*
Azara 174
  lanceolata 175
  microphylla 175, 235, *235*

B

Ballyedmond, Lord and Lady 230, 233
bamboos 18, 34, 117, 153, *237*, 238, 241
bananas 19, 239
Bardgett, Matthew 40
Barr, Hugh 9, 207, 209, 211
Beamish, Sally 66
bean
  'Green Windsor' 145
  'Painted Lady' 145
  'Viola de Cornetto' 51
Beauhill **207–211**
beech 145, 188, 228
Berberis 137
  dictyophylla 136
  'Harlequin' 28
  'Rose Glow' 28
  thunbergii
    'Aurea' 28
    f. *atropurpurea* 40
    'Atropurpurea Nana' 40
Beschorneria yuccoides 23
Betula 137, 145, 244
  ermanii 'Grayswood Hill' 125
  pendula 223
  utilis 223
    var. *jacquemontii 73*, *77*, 163, 204
      'Inverleith' *243*
      'Jermyns' *73*, *79*
birch see *Betula*
blackthorn 145
bluebells 117, 142, *142*, 182
Bonvoison, Simon 132
Borago officinalis 187
Brackenburn **153–7**
Brahea armata 18
Braithwaite, Chris 196, 197, 199
Braithwaite, Sarah 196
Brantwood 8, **65–71**
Brathay Hall 99
Bray, Charles *159*
British Pteridological Society 6, 147
broccoli, purple sprouting 145
Brockhole 9, **100–105**
Brown, Dick 73
Brown, Kath 73–5, 77, 79, 97
Brunnera
  macrophylla
    'Jack Frost' *93*, *93*
    'Variegata' ('Dawson's White') 171
Brussels sprout 'Peer Gynt' 145
Buchanan, Jim 12
Buckbarrow House **248**
Buddleja 112, 144, *186*
  alternifolia 174
  caryopteridifolia 136
  globosa 137, 182, 187
Bulbinella angustifolia 210
Busbridge, Stephen 219–20, 223
Butia capitata 239
Buxus 83

C

Cairnbeck **243–7**
Callicarpa bodinieri var. *giraldii* 'Profusion' 235, *235*
Callistemon 104, 207
Camassia leichtlinii 'Caerulea' 202, 205
Camellia 14, 84, 109, 112, *114*, 148, 179
  'Spring Festival' 85
  × *williamsii* 83, 155
    'Donation' *106*, 139, 247
Campanula 75, 161, 216
  lactiflora 77
Candelabra primulas *34*, 163, 247
Canna 18, 239
  indica 'Purpurea' *43*
  'Musifolia' 23
Cardew Lodge **248**
Cardiocrinum 123
  giganteum 15, 125, 193
    var. *yunnanense 188*, 193
Carex riparia 'Variegata' *135*
Carlyle, Thomas 181
Carpenteria californica 83, 99, *173*, 174
Cassinia 83
Castanea sativa 217
Cautleya spicata 188, 193
Cavendish, Lord and Lady 11–15
Cedrus 188
  atlantica 'Glauca' 123, 223
  libani 217
Celmisia 209, 245
  coriacea var. *semicordata* 246, 247, *247*
  sessiliflora 211
Ceonothus 182
  thysiflorus 'Skylark' 187, *187*
Cercis canadensis 'Forest Pansy' *93*, *93*, *125*
Chadwell, Chris 193
Chamaerops humilis 22
Chambers, Agnes 161
Chapelside **201–5**
Chelone 104
chives 187
Choisya ternata 'Sundance' 28
chrysanthemums 223
Cimicifuga see *Actaea*
Cirsium 202
Cistus 19, 201, 224
  × *purpurea* 'Alan Fradd' 229, *229*
Clark, Alan 59
Clark, Dick 135
Clark, Liz 135, 136–8, 168
Clark, Old Rectory **173–5**
Clarke, W.G. 70
Clough, Dorothy 194, 196
Codonopsis convolvulacea 211
Colchicum 174
Coleus 223
Collingwood, W.G. 70
Collins, Clive 177, 179
Colocasia esculenta 19
Cook, John 252
Coprosma 207
Copt Howe **119–25**
Corby Castle 8, **230–35**
Cordyline australis 70, 239
Cornus 145
  alba 'Aurea' 51
  alternifolia 123
  controversa 'Variegata' *98*, 99, 223
  'Eddie's White Wonder' 79
  mas 'Aurea' *79*, *79*
  nuttallii 155, 157, *157*
Corokia 207
Corydalis 245
  elata 139, *139*
Corylopsis pauciflora 85
Cosmos 217
Cotinus
  coggygria 'Royal Purple' 40
  'Grace' 28, 31
Cotoneaster 62
  frigidus 'Cornubia' 137
  horizontalis 187

salicifolius 'Rothschildianus' 137
  × *suecicus* 'Coral Beauty' 137
cowslips 142, *142*, 174, 223, *223*
crab apple see *Malus*
Crinodendron 104
  hookerianum 175, *175*
Crocus 15, 174
Crowder, Chris 43, *43*, 47–8, 51
Crowther, J.S. 95
Cumbria, growing conditions 6, 8
Cyathea dealbata 23
cycads *17*, 19
Cycas revoluta 19
Cyclamen 123
Cynara cardunculus 171
Cynoglossum 213

D

Dactylorhiza 123, 125, 244
  foliosa 174
daffodils see *Narcissus* (daffodils)
Dahlia 17, 18
  'Bishop of Llandaff' *43*
  'Grenadier' 23
  imperialis 23
  'Sylvia' 23
Dalemain 8, **165–71**
Daphne 190, 245
  bholua 245
    'Jacqueline Postill' 79
  mezereum 247
    f. *alba* 175
  tangutica 175
Darmera peltatum 73
Dasylirion 18
Davidia involucrata var. *vilmoriniana* 99
Davidian, David 59
Davies, Ron 188, 190–91, 192
Dean, Old Rectory **173–5**
Denby, Jonathan 9, 17, 19, 22, 23
Desfontainia spinosa 99, 104
Desmodium tiliifolium 99, *99*
Deutzia 174
Dianella 208
Dianthus 161
  'Pike's Pink' 229, *229*
Dicentra 142
Dicksonia antarctica 23, 89, *89*, 239, 241
Dierama 188, 190–91
  igneum 163
  pulcherrimum 'Blackbird' 163
Digitalis
  ferruginea 163
  × *mertonensis* 163
  purpurea 163
  purpurea 'Alba' 229
dill 199
Diocese of Carlisle 130, 132
dogwood see *Cornus*
Dracophyllum milliganii 208
Dryopteris
  affinis 'Cristata Angustata' 151, *151*
  wallichiana 151
Dunlop, John 95

E

Echium
  pininana 19, 23, *23*
  wildpretii 23
elder see *Sambucus*
Elaeagnus × *ebbingei* 85
Eleutherococcus sieboldianus 119
Ellwood, Christine 153, 154, 155, 157
Ellwood, Derek 153, 157
Embothrium coccineum 15, 104, 155, 157, 174
  'Norquinco' 125
Enkianthus 137
Ensete
  ventricosum
    'Maurelii' 19, 23
    'Montbeliardii' 19
Epimedium 155, 157
Eranthus hyemalis 192, 235, *235*
Eremurus
  himalaicus 216
  robusta 213
Erica
  arborea 85
    'Albert's Gold' 83
  canaliculata 85

Erodium 175
Eryngium 202, *204*
  alpinum 199
Erythronium 149, 155, 174
  'Pagoda' 235
Eucalyptus gunnii 113
Eucomis 190
  comosa 87, 93
Eucryphia 56, 85, 109, 155, 174, 179, 207, 244, 252
  at Holker Hall 14, 15
  cordifolia 63, *63*
  glutinosa 182, 187
  lucida × *cordifolia* 79
  × *nymansensis* 187, 211
    'Nymansay' 15, 247
Eupatorium 34
Euphorbia 18, 75, 142
  mellifera 70, 163
  myrsinites 163, *163*
  schillingii 163
  'Silver Swan' 139
Exochorda × *macrantha* 'The Bride' 157

F

Fagus
  sylvatica
    Atropurpurea Group 188
    'Dawyck Gold' 228
    var. *heterophylla* 188
      'Aspleniifolia' 228
    'Zlatia' 228
Fargesia robusta 241
Fascicularia bicolor 19, 93, *93*
Feijoa sellowiana see *Acca sellowiana*
Fellside **177–9**
fennel 199, 205, *221*
Ferdinanda eminens 23
ferns 6, 34, 55, 67, 89, 109, *155*, 238, 245
  at Scarthwaite 147, 149, 151, *151*
  at Pear Tree Cottage 28, 31
field maple 145
Filipendula 80
Fish, Margery 148
Fisher, Adrian 149
Fitzgerald, Edward 181
Fleming, Sir Daniel 126
le Fleming, Lady Diana 126
Foeniculum
  vulgare 199, 205
    'Purpureum' *221*, 229
forget-me-nots *13*, 117, *117*
foxgloves 142, 163, 223, 229, 248
Fritillaria 142, 149, 174
  meleagris 202, 205, 211
  persica 93
Fryer, Susan 104
Fryer-Spedding, John 181, 182, 184, *184*, 187
Fuchsia 'Empress of Prussia' 28

G

Gaddum, Henry 100
Galanthus (snowdrops) 117, 123, 142, 149, 157, 217, 223, 245
  'Sam Arnott' 211
Galax urceolata 211
Galium odoratum 136
Garth House 9, **237–41**
Gatesgarth **248**
Geranium 75, 104, 142, 202, *204*, 216
  'Ann Folkard' 205, *205*
  'Anne Thomson' 205
  endressii 37
    'Wargrave's Pink' 37
  × *magnificum* 37, 216
  palmatum 31
  'Patricia' 205
  phaeum 149
  sanguineum var. *striatum* 99, *99*
Gibson, Dan 8, 95, 100, 249
Gilpin, Sawrey 213
ginger lilies 18
Gladiolus 18
Glaucidium palmatum 163, *163*
Glen Artney **249**
Globba
  andersonii 19
  cathcartii 19
Gordon-Duff-Pennington, Patrick 56, 59, 62, 63
Grange Farm **140–45**

Graythwaite Hall **249**
Greencroft House **159–63**
Greening, Alec 24, 28
Greening, Linda 24, 26, 31
Gregg, Ian 140, 142, 144, 145
Gregg, Jane 140, 142, 145
Greta Hall 181
Grevillea 18, *19*, 207
Griffiths, John 111
Griffiths, Rosemary 111–14, 117
Griselinia littoralis 109
Groves, William 95
growing conditions 6, 8
Gunnera manicata 73, 83, 85, *159*, 160, *161*, 227

H

Halecat **37–40**
Halesia 13, 85, 155
  monticola 15
Hallam, Arthur 181
Hamamelis 85, 244
  mollis 235, *247*
  'Pallida' 247
Harding, Rob 140, *140*, 142
Harper, Rose 167, 168
Harvey, Jake 140, *140*, 142
Hasell, Gertrude 167
Hasell-McCosh, Jane 165, 167, 168
Haszeldine, Bob 119, 123
hawkbit 174
Hawley, John 52, 55
hawthorn 145
Hayes of Ambleside 54
Hebe 174
  buchananii 208
  haastii 208
Hedera helix f. *poetica* 148
Hedychium 18
Helleborus 15, 75, 117, 123, 142, 174, 245
  foetidus 'Wester Fisk' 229
  orientalis 125, 161, 163
Hepatica 123, 245
  × *media* 'Ballardii' 125
Hesperis matronalis 213
Hewitt, Diane 80, 83, 85
Hibberd, Shirley 18
Hicks, Nan 6, 147–9, 151
High Cleabarrow **73–9**
High Cross Lodge **87–93**, *95*
Hoheria 85, 207
Holehird *4*, 6, 77, 80, 83, 95, **95–9**
Holker Hall 8, **11–15**
Holliday, Christopher 18
holly 145
Holme Crag **32–5**
honeysuckle see *Lonicera*
hornbeam 145
Hosta 32, 75, 89, 142, *155*, 160, *161*, 204
  'Halcyon' 163, *163*
  'June' (Tardiana Group) 93
  sieboldiana 163, *213*
  'Sun Power' 79, *79*
Howard, Di 216, 217
Howard, Henry 232
Howard, Thomas 230, 231, *231*
Humulus lupulus 'Aureus' *148*
Huodendron tibeticum 13
Hutton-in-the-Forest 8, **213–17**
Hydrangea 62, 75, 85, 137, 155, 175, 252
  National Collection 83, *95*
  'Annabelle' 28
  macrophylla 'Altona' *75*
  paniculata 'Grandiflora' 157, *157*
Hymenanthera 208
Hypericum 171

I

Indigofera 174
Inglewood, Cressida, Lady 215–16, 217
Inglewood, Richard, Lord 214, 216, 217
Iris 28, *159*, 160, 204, 227
  chrysographes 'Black Knight' 175
  laevigata 135
  'Langport Wren' 229
  orchioides 190
  pseudacorus 248
  reticulata 235
  setosa 149
  sibirica 149
  unguicularis 175, 201

Irving, Maureen 159, 160, 161, 163
Irving, William 159, 161
ivies 34, 148, 235

J

Jackson, Jack and Dorothy 252
Jefferson, Kay 9, 224, 227–8, 229
Jefferson, Richard 224, 227
Jeffersonia diphylla 79
Johnson, Francis 37, *40*

K

Kalmia latifolia 179
Kerria japonica 85, *85*
King, Dorothea 167
Kingdon-Ward, Frank 58
Kinsman, David 80, 83, 85
Kirengeshoma 149
Knautia macedonica 26, 31, *204*
Kniphofia 104
  'Sunningdale Yellow' 77

L

Lake District National Park Authority (LDNPA) 103–4
Lake House **250**
Lakeland Horticultural Society 95, 96–7
Lathyrus odoratus 'Matucana' 217
Latua pubiflora 245
Laurelia serrata 63
leek 187
Lennox-Boyd, Arabella 250
Leptospermum 104, 174, 207
Leucojum vernum 157
Levens Hall 8, **43–51**
Lewisia cotyledon 247
Libertia
  ixioides 208
  peregrinans 208
Ligularia 227
  przewalskii 89
  stenocephala 89
lilies 123, 149, 247
Lingard, John 95
Linton, W.J. 65, 70
Liquidambar styraciflua 139
Liriodendron 155
  tulipifera 137
    'Fastigiatum' 99
Lobelia tupa 18
Lonicera
  fragrantissima 85
  periclymenum 'Belgica' *173*
Luzula
  sylvatica 205
    'Aurea' 139
Lysichiton
  americanum 248
  camtschatcensis 135
Lysimachia ciliata 'Firecracker' 149

M

McCosh, Sylvia 167–8
McGlasson, Stuart 251
Macleaya cordata 28, 40
Maddison, John 248
Magnolia 14, 62, 109, 112, *114*, 148, 155, 179, 244
  campbellii subsp. *mollicomata* 63
  grandiflora 241
  'Jane' *245*
  salicifolia 'Wada's Memory' 247
  sprengeri 179
  wilsonii 157, *157*
Mahonia japonica 31, *31*
Maianthemum racemosum 217
Main, John 243–6, 247
Main, Marisa 243, 244, 245, 246
Mallison, David 248
Malus
  'Carlisle Codlin' 251
  crab apple 144
  'Egremont Russet' 251
  'Keswick Codling' *181*
  'Lady's Finger of Lancaster' 196
  'Lemon Square' 196
  transitoria 99
maples see *Acer*

marjoram *204*, 205
Matthew How 8, **111–17**
Mawson, Thomas *4*, 8–9, 95, 100, 130, 249, 252
Meconopsis 123, 160, 163, *202*, 248
  cambrica 34
  grandis 168, *170*, 171
  'Lingholm' 125, 139, *139*, *243*, 247
Melianthus major 19, 93, 217, *217*
Melicytus 208
Melliodendron xylocarpum 13
Metasequoia 244
  glyptostroboides 'Gold Rush' 125
Milium effusum 'Aureum' 205
Mill House 9, **224–9**
Mirehouse **181–7**
Morina longifolia 229
Morland House **250**
Mosla dianthera 193, *193*
mosses *80*, 85
Muncaster Castle 8, **56–63**
myrtle *19*, *173*

N

Narcissus (daffodils) 113, 174, 194, *201*, 202, 248
  pseudonarcissus 139
  'Sun Disc' *245*
National Collections
  Aruncus 80
  Astilbe 80
  ferns 55
  Filipendula 80
  Hydrangea 83, *95*
  Styracaceae 13
National Trust 52, 106, 194
Nectaroscordum siculum 87, 93
Nemesia 'Confetti' *30*
Nerine 104, 190
Nigella damascena 223, *223*
Noblett, Henry 96
Nomocharis 123, 125
Nothofagus 56
  betuloides 58, 63
Nunwick Hall **219–23**
Nyssa sylvatica 'Wisley Bonfire' 244

O

Oemleria cerasiformis 205, *205*
Old Rectory **173–5**
Olea europaea 240
Olearia 207
Omphalodes
  cappadocica 'Cherry Ingram' 175
  nitida 175
Orchant, Linda 87
Orchant, Sidney 87
Origanum vulgare 'Aureum' *204*, 205
Osmanthus 148, 155
  delavayi 160
Osmunda
  regalis 31, 147
    'Cristata' 31
    'Purpurascens' 31
Osteospermum 227
oxe-eye daisies 174, 202
Oxydendrum arboreum 15
Ozothamnus 83, 174

P

Pachystegia insignis 208
Paeonia 215
  'Bowl of Beauty' 241
  delavayi 235
  lactiflora 'Solange' *239*
  mlokosewitschii 40
  officinalis 161
  'Sarah Bernhardt' 241
palms 18, 22, *89*, 93, *207*, 239, 240
Paraquilegia anemonoides 211, *211*
Parcey House **135–9**
Parthenocissus tricuspidata 235
Paxton, Joseph 251
Pear Tree Cottage **24–31**
Penstemon 54, 104, 223, *223*
  'Raven' 28
peonies see *Paeonia*
Perovskia
  atriplicifolia 174
  'Blue Spire' 175, *175*

Philadelphus
   'Belle Etoile' 193, *193*
   coronarius 'Aureus' 40
Phillips, Noel McGrigor 194
Phlomis italica 224
Phlox 245, 246
Phoenix canariensis 87, 240, *240*
Phormium 70, 87, 201, *209*
   tenax 'Variegatum' 93
Phyllostachys vivax f. *aureocaulis* 241, *241*
Physocarpus opulifolius 'Diabolo' 28
Physoplexis comosa 211
Picea
   breweriana 123
   orientalis 'Skylands' 123
   pungens 'Hoopsii' 123, *125*
Pieris 155
pinks 227, 229, *229*
Pinus aristata 123
Piptanthus nepalensis 99
Pittosporum 174, 207
   tobira 18
     'Nana' 18
Podachaenium eminens 23
Polemonium 216
   'Sonia's Bluebell' 28
Pollock, Barbara 188, 190
Pollock, David 188, 190
Pollock, Jane 188, 190
Polygonatum biflorum 171, *171*
Polystichum
   aculeatum 151, *151*
   commune 85, *85*
   formosa 85
   munitum 151
   setiferum 'Plumosum Bevis' 151
Pontederia cordata 34
poppies 142, 161, *213*
Populus tremula 63, *63*
potato, 'King Edward' 145
Potentilla 174
   'Gibson's Scarlet' 235
primroses 142, 229, *229*
   see also Primula
Primula 28, 62, 149, 155, *159*, 160, 175, *191*, 227, 248
   Bartley hybrids *135*
   florindae 175, 204
   japonica 161
   pulverulenta 161
   see also Candelabra primulas; cowslips; primroses
Prunus
   'Collingwood Ingram' *75*
   serrula 125, 163
   'Shirotae' 54, *55*
   × *yedoensis* 155, 157
Pterostyrax 13
Pulmonaria 'Blue Ensign' 93
Purdom, William 99
Pyrethrum roseum 161
Pyrus salicifolia 'Pendula' *13*, 40, 155

Q

Quarry Hill House **250**
Queen, Janet 251
Quercus
   coccinea 139, 228
   rubra 228
Quick, Sadie 248

R

Ramsden, Sir John 58, 59
Ranunculus
   aconitifolius 85
   acris 'Citrinus' 136
   ficaria 'Brazen Hussy' 136, 139, *139*
raspberry 187
Ratcliffe, Dorothy Una (DUR) 194, 196
Raven, Faith 37
Reynolds, James 201
Rhinanthus minor 202
Rhododendron 14, 56, 83, 148, *155*, 238, 248, 252
   at Matthew How 112, 113, *114*
   at Muncaster Castle 56, 58–9, *59*, *62*, 63
   at Stagshaw 106, 109, *109*
   arboreum 11, 71, *71*, 153
   'Bashful' *243*
   beanianum 63
   'Broughtonii' 58
   campanulatum *177*
   'Crest' *177*
   davidsonianum 177
   'Dusty Miller' *138*

   edgeworthii 252
   'Elizabeth' *177*
   falconeri 182, 232
   flinckii 179
   'Grenadier' 182
   'Hinode-giri' *56*
   'Hinomayo' *56*
   hodgsonii 63
   'Joan Ramsden' 58
   johnstoneanum 63
   leptocladon 62
   leucaspis 63
   Loderi Group *15*, 123
   'Loderi King George' *15*, *177*
   luteum 56
   maddenii subsp. *maddenii* Polyandrum Group 63
   orbiculare 177
   pachysanthum 179
   'Pink Pearl' *135*
   polyandrum 63, 252
   ponticum 214, 216
   schlippenbachii 79
   sino-grande 63
   'Songbird' 187, *187*
   spinuliferum 63, *63*
   'Teddy Bear' 179
   thomsonii 109
   'Vienna' 182
   yakushimanum *137*, 139
Ribes odoratum 40
Richardson, Tim 149
Rickards-Collinson, Tony and Edwina 250
Robinia pseudoacacia 34
Robinson, William 23, 167
Rodgersia 155
   podophylla 149
Romneya coulteri 174
Rosa 75, 168, 179, 202
   'Altissimo' *174*
   'Bobbie James' *100*, *148*
   'Bonica' *77*
   'Boule de Neige' *174*
   brunonii 193
   'Cerise Bouquet' 171
   'Compassion' *30*
   'Crown Princess Margareta' 31, *31*
   'Debutante' *95*
   English roses *48*, *50*
   'Fritz Nobilis' *37*
   'Goldfinch' *30*
   'Ispahan' *79*
   'Lady Hillingdon' *173*
   'Madame Alfred Carrière' *174*
   'Meg' *173*
   'Mister Lincoln' 235
   moyesii 'Geranium' 99, *99*
   × *odorata*
     'Mutabilis' 235
     'Pallida' 171
   'Paul's Himalayan Musk' 217, *217*, 229
   pimpinellifolia 'Dunwich' 174
   'Rambling Rector' 28, *95*
   'Roseraie de l'Haÿ' 171, *171*
   'Sombreuil' *174*
   'Treasure Trove' 174
Roscamp, Martin *148*
Roscoea 34, 190, 245
   alpina 193
   cautleyoides 247
Rose Castle **251**
Roundhill **251**
rowan *see* Sorbus
runner bean 'Painted Lady' 145
Ruskin, John 8, 65–6, 67, 70
Rydal Hall *4*, 8, 9, **126**, **130–32**
Rydal Mount 8, **126–30**, *132*

S

Salix alba var. *sericea* 51
Salvia
   bulleyana 191
   hians 191
   involucrata 193, *193*
   nilotica 191
   przewalskii 191
Sambucus
   nigra 144
     'Black Lace' 28
   racemosa 'Sutherland Gold' 99
Sandys, Myles 249
Sandys, Thomas 249
Sanguinaria canadensis 211
Sanguisorba canadensis 'Plena' 205

Sarcococca 85, 157
   confusa 175
Scarthwaite **147–51**
Schill, Harry 251
Schizostylis 104, 117
   coccinea 117
   f. *alba* 175
   'Major' 175
   'Viscountess Byng' 175
Scilla sibirica 187
Sebergham, Mill House 9, **224–9**
Sedum 104
   spectabile 'Autumn Joy' 187
Selinum wallichianum 199
Severn, Joan 65–6, 71
Sherriff, George 58, 168, 171
Silene
   dioica 136
   'Flore Pleno' 161
Sisyrinchium striatum 'Variegatum' 28
Sizergh Castle **52–5**
Skimmia 148, 155
Smith, Jane 149
snowdrops 117, 123, 142, 149, 160
Solanum crispum 54, 83
Solomon's seal 171, *171*
Sorbaria sorbifolia 28
Sorbus 62, 137, 244
   aria 'Hostii' 149
   aucuparia 147
Southey, Robert 181
Spedding, James 181
Spedding, John 181
Spedding, Tom 181
squash 145, *145*
Stachys byzantina 204, 205
Stagshaw **106–9**
Stanley, Fortune 37, 40
Stephanandra tanakae 28, 31
Stewartia 85
   pseudocamellia 15, 188
     Koreana Group *15*
Stipa
   arundinacea 205
   gigantea 31, 40, 229
Strelitzia reginae 18, 23
Styraceae 13
Styrax 13, 15, 85
   japonica 15
Symphytum × *uplandicum* 'Variegatum' 171, *171*
Syringa × *josiflexa* 'Bellicent' *147*, 157

T

Tate, David 9, 237–40, 241
Taxodium distichum 188
Telopea 104
Tennyson, Alfred, Lord 181, 184
Thalictrum 161, 217, *217*
   aquilegiifolium 161
   rochebruneanum 31
Thomas, Graham Stuart 196
Thomas, Margaret 96
Thompson, Jo 219, 220, 221, 223
Thompson, Myles 219
Thompson, Richard Heywood 219
Thompson, Robert 194
thymes 227
Tiarella polyphylla 31
Tilia
   × *europaea* 250
   platyphyllos 217
Tithonia rotundifolia 'Torch' *23*
Tomlinson, David and Jean 249
topiary *111*, 113–14, 117, *155*, 213, *215*
   see also Levens Hall
Trachycarpus fortunei 22, 89, 93, *207*, 239
tree ferns 23, 89, *89*, 239, 241
Tricyrtis 204, 244
Trillium 123, 149, 174, 244
   grandiflorum 117, *117*, 125, 211
Trollius 40, 202
   × *cultorum* 135
Tropaeolum
   speciosum 125
   tricolor 211
tulip tree *see* Liriodendron
tulips *13*, 18, *114*, 117, 142, *142*, 159, 202
   'Apeldoorn' *48*
   'Ballerina' *216*
   'Orange Emperor' *216*
   'Queen of Night' 28, 47, *51*
   'Uncle Tom' *216*
   'West Point' *216*
   'White Triumphator' *43*, 47, *47*, *51*

U

Ulmus glabra 'Jacqueline Hillier' *119*
umbellifers 199
Uvularia 149

V

Veratrum 155
Verbascum 89
   chaixii 'Album' 24, 28
Verbena
   bonariensis 229
   rigida 47, *47*, 51
Veronicastrum virginicum 'Apollo' 28
Viburnum × *bodnantense* 'Dawn' 85, *85*, *147*
Viola 75
violets 117
Vitis vinifera 'Purpurea' 51
Voysey, C.A. 8

W

Walpole, Hugh 153
water lilies *32*
Watson, Jack 32, 34–5
Weldenia candida 211, *211*
Wellingtonia 188
Wheeler, Bill 173, 175
Wheeler, Guy 173
Wheeler, June 173, 174, 175
willow 51, 145
Wilson, Paul 11–12
Winderwath **188–91**
Windy Hall **80–85**
Wisteria 105
   macrobotrys 209
Wood Ghyll **252**
Wood Hall **252**
Woodhouse, Charles and Margaret 250
Wordsworth, William 8, 126–30, 181
Wrathall, Joe 123

Y

yellow rattle 202
yew 113, 114, 145, 163, *216*
Yewbarrow House 9, **17–23**, 23
Yucca 52, 87, 248
   gloriosa 240